DON'T BULLSH*T YOURSELF!

DON'T BULLSH*T YOURSELF!

CRUSH THE EXCUSES THAT ARE HOLDING YOU BACK

Jon Taffer

PORTFOLIO/PENGUIN

Portfolio/Penguin
An imprint of Penguin Random House LLC
375 Hudson Street
New York, New York 10014

Most Portfolio books are available at a discount when purchased in quantity
for sales promotions or corporate use. Special editions, which include personalized
covers, excerpts, and corporate imprints, can be created when purchased in
large quantities. For more information, please call (212) 572-2232 or e-mail
specialmarkets@penguinrandomhouse.com. Your local bookstore can also assist
with discounted bulk purchases using the Penguin Random House corporate
Business-to-Business program. For assistance in locating a participating retailer,
e-mail B2B@penguinrandomhouse.com.

Library of Congress Cataloging-in-Publication Data
Names: Taffer, Jon, author.
Title: Don't bullsh*t yourself! :
crush the excuses that are holding you back / Jon Taffer.
Other titles: Don't bullshit yourself!
Description: New York, NY: Portfolio/Penguin, [2018]
Identifiers: LCCN 2017028735| ISBN 9780735217003 (hardcover) |
ISBN 9780735217010 (ebook) | ISBN 9780525536437 (international edition) |
Subjects: LCSH: Success in business. | Success. | Excuses. | Failure (Psychology)
Classification: LCC HF5386 .T119125 2018 | DDC 650.1—dc23
LC record available at https://lccn.loc.gov/2017028735

Printed in the United States of America
5 7 9 10 8 6 4

Book design by Daniel Lagin

This book is dedicated to my muse . . . my amazing wife, Nicole, who always *believed and never doubted . . . even when I did.*

Contents

DON'T BULLSH*T YOURSELF!

Introduction

*

I DON'T EMBRACE EXCUSES,
I EMBRACE SOLUTIONS

"I believe that every right implies a responsibility; every opportunity, an obligation; every possession, a duty."

—**John D. Rockefeller, American oil magnate**

The worst excuse I have made in my life haunts me to this day. When my mother died in July 2012, we were together and had had no unresolved issues for many years. However, there was a five-year period when we didn't speak. What precipitated that silence was an argument about something so trivial that I can't even remember what it was. For five years I made excuses about why I couldn't—or wouldn't—call her. Yvette Taffer was old-school—she would stand on ceremony so that it was up to me, her son, to make the first move. And I didn't want to do it. I was stubborn, but really I had no courage. I created meaningless excuses like "It's the principle of the thing," or "I won't compromise my dignity." I was just bullshitting myself. What a waste of time, energy, resources, and love! We *all* have to stop bullshitting ourselves.

Fortunately, I came to my senses, albeit five years too late. One day my brother, Lewis, and I were talking about an upcoming family event that my mom would be attending. As we talked, something in me just clicked. I finally realized what a jerk I had been all those years. Right then I picked up the phone and called my mother, apologizing profusely and feeling like a fool for wasting years we could have spent together. Waiting those five years to make that call is one of my biggest regrets.

The time we lose to excuses is devastating. No one loved me more than my mother did. The woman who gave birth to me, nurtured me, protected me, and fed and clothed me—no argument is worth abandoning that person. Listen to me: Excuses hurt, they leave wounds and can scar. They are your enemy. They steal the future and can destroy you. Not calling my mother wasted precious time. Time, as you will learn in this book, is the most powerful thing we have. When we do not use it correctly, as was the case with my mother, it can hurt us for years.

I have witnessed the destruction excuses wreak every day. As a business professional for more than three decades, I have been in the unique and privileged position to see firsthand what excuses do to people. Long before *Bar Rescue* became a television phenomenon, I was helping to fix broken businesses and owners. The root cause of all the problems I saw were excuses. I can walk into any unsuccessful business or talk to a person who has been unable to fulfill a single dream and see the results of a series of poor decisions that got them to a bad place. The stench of failure hangs in the air like stale cigar smoke. Talk to the people behind the failures, and you often find that they are overachievers at explaining

2

disappointment away with what they think are logical reasons. They are masters of bullshitting themselves. I've heard every outlandish and hackneyed excuse in the book—from "I have no time to check my company books" to "I can't make my business in New Jersey a success because taxes are too high," or "There's turmoil in the Middle East and Ukraine, so I just can't think about trying to succeed" to "My cat died." Come on!

Excuse makers seem to put more time into crafting the perfect justification for their actions (or inactions) than into working and succeeding. But let's be real—it's not just owners of struggling bars who make excuses. We all do. And it's time for us to stop. In the short term, an excuse seems like an easy fix. It's anything but. Psychologists call excuse making "rationalization," a defense mechanism we use to justify bad behavior and poor decisions. While the excuses seem perfectly rational to the excuse maker, everyone else is rolling their eyes. Excuse making is just a form of lying. When you make an excuse you're holding yourself back! Why would you do that? *Don't Bullsh*t Yourself* teaches you how to identify and face those lies head-on, and turn them around into positive action.

Excuses are the common denominator of failure.

In my experience, they fall into six major categories, which we will go through in this book together to bust each one: fear, knowledge, time, circumstances, ego, and scarcity. I chose these six because they have come up repeatedly during my thirty years of working with failing businesses, failing owners, and failing people, and when facing my own excuses that had the potential to derail me. Each chapter centers on one of these types of excuses, revealing its facets and manifestations. You might notice some overlapping themes. That's because the emotions that underpin excuses—unhappiness, frustration, and discontent—cause the excuses to feed on each other. We're going to break that up.

I'm here to help. I've seen the power of people confronting their own excuses and turning their businesses and lives around, including my own. From people who defied the odds, resisting the temptation to make excuses, to those who struggled with excuse making and were not able to resist the temptation, we'll explore their instructive and inspiring stories in the pages to come. So don't shy away; it's time to grab this book and identify your own excuse-making bad habits, and then let's work together to change them with actionable steps. My goal with *Don't Bullsh*t Yourself* is for you to become accountable every single day for every decision you make and action you take.

Your excuses are lies, illusions, delusions, traps, and mirages; they are all holes we dig—and then jump right into. I reject excuses and embrace solutions. When I'm done with you, you will too.

In college, I studied cultural anthropology and saw that behavior in primates isn't so different from our own. This anthropology background has helped me to understand people at their core—what motivates them and what doesn't. At the end of the day, we're all responding to stimuli just as our ancestors, the cavemen, did, and very similar to how animals in the jungle do when it comes to protecting their own territory. From my experience helping bars, restaurants, nightclubs, and hotels survive and thrive, I am a grassroots expert on human behavior. It is easy to change a business; it's hard to change people. Yet it's not impossible. One way to do it is to learn how to see an excuse for what it is (a false premise), identify the real issue underlying the excuse making, and address it in a straightforward, unemotional way. You've seen me do it on TV.

In fact, on *Bar Rescue*, when I deal with an excuse maker, the first thing I do is feel out his emotional hot buttons and points of pride. If I choose to attack his pride—*"This place is a mess, it sucks"*—often he will stand up like a gorilla pounding on his chest and say, *"I'm better than this."* Does that motivate him to change? I always hope it will, but, unfortunately, in many situations it doesn't.

So I switch to fear. *"What happens when your business closes? What happens when you go broke? What happens when you're bankrupt?"* I try to scare the shit out of him. Sometimes, if he has kids, I'll even mention them. *"Is this the way you want your children to live? Are you going to have the money to buy them food, let alone send them to college?"* I hope that triggers him to think, *Wow, maybe I'm wrong. Maybe I need to change things.* One way or another, I have to get him to that state of mind.

My third tactic, and the one I unfortunately use the most, is confrontation. When there's no choice, I go at him like a classic drill sergeant and break him down. I beat on him until the moment comes when he doubts himself, and in that second his mind will open up and he'll say, *"Wow, you might be right, I might be wrong."* In that fleeting moment, with his brain open a crack, I can walk right in.

Then he is ready to take a hard look at the deception of his excuses, and the fact that the only person he's fooling is himself. Most of the time my clients have a lightbulb moment at this point. Now, only after this revelation, we can get to work on dismantling the lies within their excuses, and then work on dismantling the excuses and the behavior. The minute they take responsibility, everything changes. Once they're in a humble position, they really can see the absurdity of the stories they tell.

We're going to get there—together. To do so means shifting your mind-set, consciously doing uncomfortable things, taking a risk, confronting your lies, and asking for help. You must be willing to make the changes necessary to turn your life from excuse filled to one in which you are going after what's really important and not letting anything stand in your way. Unless you embrace solutions and do the work necessary to cut through your own crap, you will never win at business or in life. This book gives you a chance to confront your own baloney and get back to winning.

Excuses hold back the person who feels like she is drowning in her business or her job. It's an illusion! Delusions, dishonesties, and foolishness control excuse makers even though in most cases *they know better.* They are genuinely scared—the fear isn't fake. That's why diagnosing failure is so easy. If I can turn that lie around and see it for what it is (you're actually not too busy, you actually don't need more money than you have), and then change the words they use to describe the real issue, I can change their lives. Without a doubt, every perceived problem can be turned into a genuine opportunity for growth.

If your business is failing, *it is only because of you.* Someone else is succeeding in the same position and under similar conditions. If you own the failure and truly blame yourself, you will fight it. If you blame an excuse or someone else, you have no reason to change and will continue to fail. No excuses! Own your failure and you will own your success.

As much as I'd like to, I can't help everyone in person. That's one of the reasons why I wrote this book. The lessons in *Don't Bullsh*t Yourself* apply to business owners, those starting a business or thinking of starting one, individuals who are working their way up in a company or want to leave it, and those who simply want to change bad habits that hold them back from succeeding at life. As I said earlier, I've broken up the chapters into the six types of excuses I have heard the most often for more than thirty years. Each chapter defines the excuse, gives examples, provides ways to change the excuse into a solution, and offers personal stories of those who have conquered it and created great success in their lives. You'll find profiles of people I call Bullsh*t Busters, those individuals who have unique and powerful stories that are also very relatable and inspiring. I approach the problem of excuses as I do in "real life," hoping to get the same result for you if you are serious about your future and willing to keep reading and push through the discomfort that will come with recognition. At the end of each chapter you'll find a DBY (Don't Bullsh*it Yourself) To-Do List. It's a short action-oriented inventory for busting up your excuses and embracing solutions.

If your business or your life is in trouble or not growing as much as you'd like, once I can get you to recognize the excuses you make, I can build you back up with a way to change them into solutions. After more than 150 episodes of *Bar Rescue,* I've learned that once I break a person down and his mind is open, he realizes that there's benefit in change. Moment to moment, he needs that pat on his back, he needs encouragement, and the person who taught him he's wrong (me) has to tell him he can be right.

Once I show you your own excuses and lay them bare, I offer you actionable ways of dealing with them, as well as insights and experiences from people just like you who have been on the tightrope of excuses and made it to the platform without falling into the net. You can do this too. The examples and practical strategies I'll show you in this book will help you learn to change your excuses into solutions—for good. If you stop the excuses, embrace solutions, and become more action oriented, what do you think that will mean for your future? Here's what I think it will mean:

* *You'll recognize your power.* Tackling excuses and actively finding solutions clearly demonstrates you're smarter, stronger, and savvier than you probably give yourself credit for.
* *You'll learn more.* Orienting yourself toward solutions is a great teacher.
* *You'll accomplish more.* Excuses waste *a lot* of time and eat up valuable resources.
* *You'll have more fun.* Excuse making is a downer. When you stop, life gets less anger provoking, you'll become more engaged in the moment, and you'll start to enjoy life in the present.
* *You'll make more money.* Excuses can drain or stagnate your bank account. When you are solving problems, making changes, taking actions, and evolving your life and business, prosperity follows!
* *You'll have more power.* Simply put, the more you accept responsibility for things that happen in your life, the more control and influence you will have over your future.

It's time to stop excusing your life away. It's time to stop blaming the economy, the government, a new competitor, or even construction on the street. It's time to stop bullshitting yourself! We fail only because of ourselves. The minute you take responsibility, everything changes. Let's embrace some solutions.

Chapter 1

*

EXCUSE #1:
FEAR

"Inaction breeds doubt and fear. Action breeds confidence and courage. If you want to conquer fear, do not sit home and think about it. Go out and get busy."

—Dale Carnegie, American writer and lecturer

Excuses Based on Apprehension and Anxiety

We begin at the beginning, with the mother of all excuses: fear of failure. This can mean fear of hurting someone else's feelings, fear of how you will feel if things don't work out exactly as you planned, fear of ridicule and criticism, fear of what could happen when you screw up, and, yes, even fear of how your life will change if you succeed. Fear provides a convenient comfort zone for many people. If you're afraid to do something, it's safer to avoid it, right? No way. It's time to change your perspective and confront that fear head-on.

I know fear. I can relate to it. I've made stupid investments. I've made stupid decisions as an employee and as a manager. I've been fired. I've lost businesses. But I also know fear can be the most powerful tool to make me take action. Fear can be a great motivating factor, and I try to use it to help other people overcome their fears. When someone refuses to acknowledge she has to do something to save herself or her job, I switch on the fear gear. *"What happens when the place closes? What happens if you go broke? What happens when you're bankrupt?" Get going and do something to prevent any of these things from happening.* That is a key lesson about fear—use it, don't succumb to it!

Fear is part of human nature. Everyone experiences it. In fact, if someone was chasing you down a dark street, you'd probably be terrified. You'd run as fast as you could. In that sense, fear is a vital response to acute situations that present real danger. So it's a delicate balance to acknowledge fear and then figure out how to act. Don't use fear as an excuse to avoid situations that may present some risk or as an opportunity to cling to comfortable routines and familiar surroundings. Right now, I ask you to look at your perceived fears rationally to see if there is any real basis for you to allow them to control your choices and actions. Think about how you can use that very fear to propel you forward toward a goal, one step at a time.

In the late 1980s, I entered into a business partnership with a guy who was sort of a player. He cheated on his own wife and family. When I was about to do business with the guy, a friend of mine said, "Listen, Jon. Don't do business with a guy who cheats on his own family. If he cheats on them, he'll cheat on you in a minute."

When you hear yourself saying . . .

* ✶ I'm afraid of failing.
* ✶ I'm afraid of being embarrassed and humiliated.
* ✶ What if things don't pan out?
* ✶ Others have tried this and failed.
* ✶ Trying this makes me feel scared and uncomfortable.
* ✶ What if I'm wrong?
* ✶ There aren't any guarantees.
* ✶ What if my reputation suffers?
* ✶ What if I lose the respect of my peers?
* ✶ I might not be able to start over if things don't work out.

. . . it's time to face your fears and stop bullshitting yourself!

I didn't listen and did the deal anyway. I was ripped off to the tune of six hundred thousand dollars—every dime I had. Afterward, I was scared, and I feared entering into partnerships for a long time. But I knew that partnerships can be lucrative and beneficial when two parties bring different but complementary strengths to the table. I did not want my past fear to interfere with future opportunities. I didn't want the fact that I was burned once to poison the well and prevent me from forming the right kinds of business relationships.

Today, I am careful about forming business alliances. I *do not* use fear of losing my shirt as an excuse to avoid advantageous partnerships. Instead, I carefully consider the full character of any potential partner or associate before I even think about letting him into my business and life. I do not allow fear to paralyze me; instead, it makes me strategically cautious.

The second restaurant I owned and operated, in the Mall of America, was hugely successful, achieving more than $2 million in sales in the first three months of opening! Yet in all the chaos of sale volume exceeding expectations, we lost $600,000. I ran out of money and had to find a partner to sell 50 percent of the restaurant to for just $150,000. I had no other choice. Was I afraid? Hell, yeah. But I had a family to support. It was humbling—but my fear was also motivating. Selling half of the restaurant was scary, but it was scarier to imagine doing nothing and losing the establishment completely. In just a few months, I turned the restaurant around and profited more than $800,000 that year and $1 million every year thereafter. Life-altering challenges can be frightening, but they are often the most worthwhile to meet head-on. Unchallenged fears hold you back. If you don't confront them, you get stuck.

Think about war. War is scary; there's a legitimate possibility of pain, suffering, and death. Fear of these things is real—so why is it that so few soldiers go AWOL after leaving boot camp? Soldiers are often thrown immediately into unfamiliar, dangerous situations, but they usually pull off the tasks at hand. Think about young men in World War II parachuting into Normandy, not knowing what they would find there. A few weeks earlier, they might have been working at a gas station or pushing papers behind a desk. Next thing they knew, they were jumping out of planes. They were scared shitless, but they jumped anyway. What happened to their fear?

If World War II seems too distant for you, consider the story of Marcus Luttrell.[1] In June 2005, he was part of a four-man

SEAL team that was dropped into an isolated area of Afghanistan on a mission to capture or kill Mohammad Ismail, a dangerous Taliban leader. Their mission went sour almost as soon as they hit the ground. Luttrell and his three comrades were outnumbered by dozens of heavily armed Taliban fighters, who gunned the group down. Only Luttrell survived the onslaught—he was alive, but also alone in horribly unfriendly, violent territory with serious injuries including gunshot wounds and a broken back. In his book *Lone Survivor,* Luttrell writes that he was exhausted, dying of thirst, and scared—but he carried on. The next day, he came upon a waterfall, where he was able to quench his thirst and clean his wounds, but the water did not assuage his fears. He was still very much afraid.

Luttrell says that his grueling SEAL training certainly helped him survive this horrific episode, particularly the notorious series of physically and psychologically trying exercises that take place during "hell week." Contenders crawl for miles over rough terrain and swim in an icy ocean in full combat dress. They haul heavy loads under actual gunfire, which simulates carrying a wounded buddy through a war zone. Instructors tie potentially suffocating knots in scuba gear breathing tubes, and trainees have to undo them quickly before they run out of air.

Physical and psychological fortitude gained from that period of training certainly played an important role in Luttrell's survival. Despite his injuries, he managed to elude the Taliban fighters, descend a steep gorge, cross a muddy river, and keep himself hidden for many hours. Finally, some friendly locals discovered him, brought him to their village, and gave him shelter and food until U.S. military forces could rescue him. And you're telling me you're afraid of failing or making a mistake?

Here's some news: You're going to fail. You're going to make mistakes. Both are part of the path to success in life and business—and they're rarely fatal, as they could have been in Luttrell's case.

Whatever journey you're on, it's likely that you started out with big goals and a sense of purpose. You believed in yourself, your ideas, and your own competence when you started a business or took a job. You agreed to do the work. We have to get you back to that place—where you craved success instead of fearing failure.

Think Incrementally

Luttrell can teach us something about how to conquer fear—and we don't need to go through basic training to learn the lessons.

During his training period, and especially during hell week, Luttrell noticed that the guys who looked at what was left of the training period as a whole ("I have five more days before this is all over") didn't make it to the end. They threw in the towel and left the SEALs. Those who stuck it out, like Luttrell, concentrated only on the specific task in front of them, moving from one challenge to the next as if they were individual, unrelated jobs. When Luttrell found himself stranded and hurt, he didn't think, *The only way I'm going to get away from these fighters is to crawl for miles through valleys and rivers until I'm safely hidden.* At first he thought only about getting down that ravine. Once he climbed down, he thought about crossing a river to get to the other side. He considered each step of his journey as a single undertaking. He thought in increments. If he hadn't, he would have been too overwhelmed and perhaps would have given up—and died.[2]

I had an analogous (although not life-threatening) problem

one time shooting *Bar Rescue*. Several years ago, one of my producers put the number of shoot days remaining on the whiteboard in the master control room. Each day I saw a huge number, at times higher than two hundred, written on that board. To me, this meant more than two hundred days on the road, away from home. Seeing it all day made my task overwhelming, even depressing. I had the numbers permanently removed and it worked. Without the numbers on the board, I simply focused on doing my best one day at a time.

Don't think about all the steps you need to take to get from point A to point B, from where you are now to where you want to go. Instead, try thinking about the first small step you need to take. Once you complete that, what's the next incremental move you can make? If you break down a change or process into small, accessible, and doable tasks, you won't be distracted, overwhelmed, or defeated by thinking of the monumental nature of the big picture. This works for anything you want to accomplish, from cleaning up your office to plotting your next career move. Smaller tasks are less scary than big ones and far easier to complete.

When breaking down a change or action, try to balance difficult tasks with easier ones. While Luttrell did not have a choice in his effort to remain calm and survive, his was also an acute circumstance. You will have a choice in how you view and allocate your time because an armed warrior isn't chasing you down. Lucky you.

Assess the Risk

Peter Guber, a longtime entertainment entrepreneur, chairman and CEO of Mandalay Entertainment, professor at UCLA, and owner and co-owner of three professional sports teams, among other things, says that fear can be an ally, not an adversary. To see it that way we have to get the message that fear—FEAR—is "false evidence appearing real," he wrote in the *Harvard Business Review.*[3]

In the early 1990s, well before multiplex theaters were commonplace, Guber, as chairman and CEO of Sony Pictures Entertainment, saw a lucrative opportunity to build super-multiplex theaters that would show sixteen to twenty movies at the same time. Guber knew that because it was such a brazen idea, he would likely meet resistance when presenting it to one of Sony's companies, the Loews theater group. He was right. When he went to pitch the idea of creating such a theater in a location that already had many movie houses—New York City—he was faced with a great deal of opposition; the team was afraid this type of theater would cannibalize Loews' existing business.

Guber decided to bypass the Excel spreadsheets and colorful pie charts and instead tell a story to the skeptical executives. After all, he was in the business of weaving compelling narratives. Think of the mall food court, Guber said. If one type of food sells out or is unavailable, there are ten other kinds of food to choose from and enjoy. "We should make movies that people consume emotionally with the same availability as a food court," he told them. "If the movie that brought you to the theater [was] sold out, there were 15 or 16 other movies to consume and enjoy."

The story helped the Loews team understand how real

evidence did not support their fears, but in fact demonstrated that the concept could work. I give them credit for overcoming *their* fears of cannibalizing their business and trying something new. Had they not, another theater company would have beat them to it, and they might not have had the chance to gain market share in the business. The Sony Sixty-seventh Street multiplex was built and went on to be very successful, and the multiplex is now a ubiquitous feature of most urban and suburban landscapes.

Guber could have been defeated by Loews' reaction and given up on the idea. Loews executives could have given in to their fears and outright rejected Guber's idea. You've probably been in similar situations in your own life: you have a great idea, or you want to ask for something, but you know (or you think) you will meet resistance from stakeholders (they could be your colleagues, your family, your friends, or your investors, depending on what your idea is). If you do start a new business, expand a business, ask for a raise, change jobs, or move, how high is the actual risk that your life will be ruined, your family will leave you, and you will be penniless for the rest of your life? It's obviously low, and you know that. What are the real risks, then? You might lose some money and your cash flow might be restricted for a period of time if you start a business, or you could hate a new job that seemed like it was going to be just perfect. You might find that your vision or idea sucks or needs tweaking. Of course, almost every important decision you'll ever make carries real risks. However, they are possibilities that won't ruin your life unless you allow them to.

In one bar I rescued, an attractive bartender, whom I'll call Joann, not only was a great bartender but also had excellent people and management skills. She told me she had worked at this failing bar for twelve years. *Twelve years.* "Why?" I asked her.

"You have a great presence, you're attractive, you're smart, and you are a good bartender with management skills. Why are you here?" She really didn't have a legitimate answer. "It's like family to me," she said. "If I went somewhere else, more might be demanded of me, and what if I'm not up to it?"

It seemed as if Joann preferred to wallow in mediocrity than pursue greater success even though her parachute—her skills, personality, education, experience, and background—were enough to assure a soft landing. Over a twelve-year period, Joann could have gotten a better job at a better establishment, earned promotions, and maybe even opened her own place. She would have certainly been managing one at this point if she had wanted to. Joann wasn't able to assess the real risks of taking the chance— and so had been stuck in a rut. Though her fears were real to her, they could have been overcome by thinking through the risks. I wanted her to flip her fears by having her ask herself the following questions:

* What if what is asked of me at a new job is very familiar, and because of my experience I excel at a new job in a new establishment?
* Even though I will lose my "family" at my current job, isn't it also possible that I will form new relationships and a new work family at a new job?
* Couldn't I learn new skills at a new job and build on those I have, making me even more desirable to my employer and even future employers?

Sometimes all you have to do is turn your fear into a question— and that's when you see how unrealistic or unfounded your fear really is. In Joann's case, she realized that the risk of the tasks in a new job being totally foreign to her were unrealistic. There would likely be a good balance of tasks she could do backward and forward, and others she'd have to learn. She could hit the ground running in many areas, but would have the leeway to learn what she didn't know. Moving on to new opportunities sometimes means you lose touch with people—but it doesn't have to, and real friends are not defined by whether we see them every day at work. After essentially demystifying her fears, Joann was able to assess a new job offer and accept the position, which improved her finances and work experience.

Take Corrective Action

Expect the best but plan for the worst. The most reliable way not to let an unexpected or disappointing outcome spiral out of control is to have a well-developed exit strategy or corrective action planned in advance.

Take Joann, my bartender friend. Even if she didn't take to a new job, it wouldn't be the end of her career. That is a completely unrealistic outcome. It happens sometimes that we don't like a job, but that doesn't mean we're finished. I have a friend, Fred, who took a job that looked great on paper—it was a promotion that came with a great title, many perks, and a much higher salary. The trouble is, after two weeks he hated it: the company culture didn't mesh with his personality. Do you know what he did? Fred made the best of it—and looked for another job. Once he understood he wasn't stuck, going to work wasn't painful. He did his job to the best of his ability, knowing that excelling at the new responsibilities the job offered would help him get another job. He put in a year at the job—not much in the scheme of a lifetime. He didn't burn any bridges and in fact made a couple of valuable contacts, which he kept for many years after. After a year, he found another job in a firm more suitable for him. His attitude was "Let me make any opportunity all I can and work every day to change my circumstances."

Many of us are no different from Fred because we can end up in jobs we don't like too. Let me calm your fears about this right here: if a new job doesn't turn out to be a good fit, continue to learn and develop your skills as you look for other opportunities. New skills and the successful grasp of new responsibilities look great on a résumé. As long as you stayed for substantial amounts of time at previous jobs, potential new employers aren't going to hold one short stint against you.

Check In with Yourself

So you've made a few small steps to face your fears. You have, haven't you? If not, put this book down and go! If you have, way to go! Now it's time to review your results. What have you learned? Not so scary after all—or maybe not as scary as you thought. What did you do right and what could you have done better? This process not only makes you think rationally about your decisions, it also makes you less afraid to take action the next time you face a fear that paralyzes you in some endeavor.

A crucial part of overcoming fear that may keep you from shifting course or tweaking strategies is to continually assess and examine your decision-making process. Knowing you review situations and make solid decisions builds confidence. Don't become paralyzed and therefore avoid making necessary changes to aspects of your business, job, or life that aren't working. Trial and error are pit stops on the road to success. Missteps, unexpected negative outcomes, and outright failures are nothing to be afraid of. They have been my greatest lessons and my strongest challenges to improving my character and self-confidence. So don't fear them—embrace them, learn from them, and allow them to lead you to new possibilities for success.

Consider Google. From its start in a garage in 1996 and for several years after, Google was an idea and a technology that were unprofitable and directionless outside of Internet search. For one thing, Google couldn't find a reliable and stable revenue source. It tried selling search appliances, bright yellow rack-mounted devices that provided document indexing, to businesses, as well as selling its own search technology to other search engines. Both of those enterprises failed. Founders Larry Page and Sergey Brin and the Google team assessed these mistakes and decided to abandon the failing efforts and go in an entirely new direction.

In reviewing the results, the team saw a connection between the things people search for on the Internet and the products and services that relate to those subjects. For instance, people searching for information about baby care might also want to buy baby care products. In 2000 the company launched its AdWords program, which allowed businesses to target their advertisements to people searching for specific terms on Google.[4] With this program, when someone typed "baby care" into the Google search engine, not only did many advice and medical sites pop up but also ads for all sorts of baby care products. People appreciated that the ads were not intrusive and didn't interfere with informational results. The idea and, more important, the decision to try it out despite fears the team might have had paid off. AdWords continues to comprise the bulk of Google's revenue.[5]

Bullshit Buster: Sharon Levy

Sharon was the executive vice president of original series at Spike TV. I've known her since I started on *Bar Rescue*. To me she epitomizes someone who embraces fear and works through it. It's won her a lot of success at her job, not only with *Bar Rescue* but with other highly rated programs, including *Ink Master, Auction Hunters,* and the critically acclaimed *Tut,* featuring an all-star cast led by Sir Ben Kingsley.

"Excuses come from fear," Sharon says. "I have always been someone professionally who doesn't like excuses nor when people don't take responsibility for their actions. I am big on accountability, and an important part of that has to be letting go of the fear associated with mistakes. It's okay to make mistakes; we live in a society where we forget that. Owning mistakes makes excuses unnecessary."

If you manage other people, part of helping those who work for you to get over fear of failure is allowing them to fail without overreacting or reacting in a way that encourages them to hide from it or lie. As Sharon says, "You have to let people know it is okay to fail, but that when they have made a bad decision, or something does not work out, they can say, 'Wow, I messed that up, here's what happened, it won't happen again,' and I'm not going to have a fit. That is someone I respect. I don't respect the person who covers up his or her mistakes."

If you want to make changes and have an impact on your

work—whatever it is—you need to take risks and face failure. As someone who works in the fast-changing world of TV, Sharon understands this. "I constantly remind my people not to let the larger global industry changes affect what they do every day. You can process, maneuver, adapt, and be flexible," she says. "The future is going to happen whether we like it or not. When people use larger issues as excuses, I tend to not respond well because it's an easy way out. Instead, I say, 'I am fighting like hell to make something great, and I'll protect or defend it if I know it's good.' When a show does not work, there are a million reasons why that is. You have to figure out what doesn't work and why—as well as when it *does* work and *will* work."

Despite her terrific record of success, Sharon is not immune to failure. She recalls a time when she was really excited about a show but her staff didn't share her enthusiasm for it. "I loved the title and the idea for the show, but they told me it was not executable. It wasn't until we were in postproduction when I realized they were right—it wasn't a good show. I went to my superiors immediately and said that we needed to mitigate the loss. We sheltered the show at a time slot that wouldn't kill us. My boss was great about it, in part because I didn't hide the failure from him. I owned up to it right away. Sure, that's scary—but it's scarier to pretend you didn't make what would be a very visible mistake. He said, 'I hear you.' I am lucky I work for people who say it is worth taking the risk."

Even though that particular show was a failure, if Sharon believes in a show she will still go out on a limb for it. "The worst that can happen is spectacular failure and I can be fired. It's not lovely but it's okay. I know I am good at what I do and I made a mistake but I can do something else." This simple statement shows remarkable fortitude on Sharon's part. A different kind of person might consider being fired to be a devastating loss. To understand that being fired may not be amazing but it's not the final curtain call either takes clearheadedness and feet firmly placed in reality. Sharon doesn't imbue possible outcomes, such as a termination that might result from a bad decision, with magical powers—as in "Getting fired is the worst thing that could happen so I'm going to keep my head down and not take any risks."

"If you are terrified of every moment, you won't make bold choices, which will often be the best choices," says Sharon. I have found this to be true in my own career. While it's true that sometimes an idea can sound crazy under certain circumstances, and you have to be bold if you believe in it, don't be so quick to talk yourself out of it because you're afraid. Just be prepared to accept the consequences, however they play out.

Bullshit Buster: Anthony Frasier

While I've had to overcome fear plenty of times, I've had the good fortune never to have had to because of who or what I am. However, for some, that is not the case. Because of who he is and where he is from, and being an African American in the tech field, Anthony Frasier had to face fear moving to Silicon Valley, pitching investors, and often being the only person of color in the room. Anthony is an entrepreneur now based in Newark, New Jersey. His journey was featured on the CNN documentary *Black in America*. Anthony is the founder of ABF Creative, a multicultural podcast network. He's also the cofounder of The Phat Startup, a media company that produces content for entrepreneurs working in hip-hop and urban spaces. He is also the author of *Don't Dumb Down Your Greatness—A Young Entrepreneur's Guide to Thinking and Being Great.*

Before venturing out on his own as a tech entrepreneur, Anthony worked the night shift at Kmart, unloading boxes from the back of a truck. "My motivation to explore the tech world came from a frustration when dealing with people who are comfortable in mediocre jobs. At Kmart, a lot of my coworkers had this attitude that 'This is my life, that's it, and there is nothing else, no place else to go.' I was very depressed about the lack of ambition around me," says Anthony.

One night changed his life. He remembers it like it was yesterday. A truck had arrived at the store and it was stuffed to the gills. Only three people had shown up to work that night, and even though they were willing to get the job done, the store manager was rude and nasty. Anthony had to ask himself why he was accepting this treatment. "I was nearly in tears that day. Here I was, willing to do the work of three men, yet I was spoken to and treated like I didn't matter."

At the same time that he was holding down a job at Kmart, Anthony was developing a video game in his free time, at nights and on weekends. He believed in the game and thought it was salable. His dream was to be a game developer, but there weren't many game development companies where he lived in New Jersey. That project took on a new importance after that night. "I thought, I have to change something. I had read about a conference in Los Angeles called E3, where all the top tech and game people would be." It was a huge risk, but Anthony quit his job that spring, knowing that he could not pursue selling his game to

Silicon Valley developers and still work at Kmart in New Jersey. He took some of his savings and bought a plane ticket to Los Angeles. "Sometimes people put on the brakes when they are scared, but whenever I'm afraid, I press the gas even harder and go full force to see what will happen," says Anthony. "I didn't have anything to lose at that point, so for me there was no downside to any of it."

Anthony and a friend took the video game to the conference, showed it around, made some connections, and went home. Nothing happened—and Anthony was out of a job. "I spent the summer after the conference building a Web site for my game, and making no money. I was living at home, trying to assure my mother that my project would go somewhere, and not to worry. She wanted me to get a job. I said, 'Please let me give this game a shot, it's got to work.'"

One day Anthony was perusing job postings on Craigslist, thinking that maybe he should take his mother's advice and get a job. He noticed an "Intern wanted" ad for a Web site called Bubbleline. After researching its traffic, Anthony realized that his game Web site got more traffic than Bubbleline did. "I didn't know what these people would think since I didn't have a college degree," says Anthony, "and my last job was unpacking trucks at Kmart, not working the Genius Bar at Apple."

Anthony used the energy created by his fear and apprehension to build up his nerve. He called Bubbleline, and they invited him to their offices. "I brought them the Web site I designed and the data on the traffic I had built. I told them that I might be able to do the same for them." Bubbleline liked what they saw. After a month of interning, they hired Anthony to do business development for them.

Anthony thought that the person who had invested in Bubbleline might be interested in investing in his video game. He
liked it and agreed to do it with Anthony. Now really scared,
Anthony thought, *What will happen if it doesn't work?* On Twitter
that day, Anthony learned about Accelerator, which provides mentorship, and sometimes funding and resources, to tech start-ups.
His investor urged him to fill out the application because it could
be another way to fund the project. Two weeks later, Anthony got
a phone call asking if he wanted to come out to Silicon Valley. He
wound up living in Silicon Valley for six months as part of the
Accelerator program. He succeeded in the program and they
asked him to stay and create his company in California. "I always
wanted to go back home to Newark, where I grew up," says Anthony.
"I wanted to give back and assist in improving the community
that has been so dear to me. I want to show that people can create
tech wherever they may be."

Anthony is a winner who uses his fears as currency for
improvement. "It's scary to be a young black entrepreneur because
you do not see yourself as part of the technology industry. The
examples that were out there were few and rarely visible to people
of color." He grew up in a single-parent home void of a father's
mentorship or examples of success from men. Anthony overcame
his fears by reading books on networking as well as books with
advice for men. "I spent a lot of time in my zone reading about
things a dad should teach a young man, including how to tie a tie,"
he says. "Don't dumb down your greatness," Anthony advises.
"Fear should be a motivator, not a handicap."

Remember, your fears are often fearless endeavors for others.
Anthony's fear of tying his tie is a mindless endeavor for someone
else. Television cameras are very intimidating to many people,

preventing them from simply being themselves, but I don't even think about them being there.

Anthony's strategy of using fear as a motivator is my go-to strategy when dealing with failing businesses and failing people. Let's go back to Marcus Luttrell for a moment. The coauthor of his book, Patrick Robinson, told a reporter that Luttrell was "very sad and introverted" as they worked on the manuscript.[6] Still, Luttrell soldiered on, forged ahead, and published a successful book. If he and others like him can overcome fears and carry on, *you* can certainly face fears about changing jobs, asking for a raise, or pursuing a new idea. Human beings are highly capable— give yourself some credit.

Do something that scares you *today*—and own it!

DBY To-Do List

* Think incrementally. Face fears by breaking them down into small action steps. Take one step at a time.
* Assess the risk. Ask yourself, is my fear rational? If it is rational, what is the worst that can happen if the fear is realized? Would the potential outcome be devastating or something you could handle? If it's not rational, you need to get over it now, and the best way to get over any fear is to face it and act.
* Take corrective action. Have a plan B before you make a bold move. Knowing there is a plan in place to correct any missteps facing your fears may cause—because I can't guarantee that every decision is going to have a perfect outcome—gives you some security. Having a plan means you're not going to be

caught flat-footed if something doesn't work out. You can keep moving forward.

* Check in with yourself. I think postmortems are essential. I always assess how I did after a *Bar Rescue* episode has finished shooting. I watch the show and think about how I could improve upon my own decisions for the next show. I am constantly reevaluating and assessing my actions. Facing your fears and making a bold move offer tremendous learning opportunities.

Chapter 2

*

EXCUSE #2:
KNOWLEDGE

"All men who have turned out worth anything have had the chief hand in their own education."

—Walter Scott, Scottish novelist, playwright, and poet

Excuses Based on a Lack of Information or a False Sense of Superior Wisdom

Too often on *Bar Rescue* or in my consulting work, owners do not know how to use their POS (point of sale) system, the basics of inventory management, or other simple tasks. To them, this knowledge is beneath them, or for their management to learn. These are the owners who are unaware that employees are stealing cash and products from them, or who have employees who disrespect their products and don't know it. These are the owners who are held hostage by their managers but never learn more in order to make changes. Then, when they fail and close, they blame it on "management."

The beliefs that there's nothing new to learn, that certain knowledge is beneath your pay grade, and that you are not capable of learning new things (for whatever reason) are complete bullshit. Those excuses are really about *you* not taking full responsibility for *your* job or business.

This type of excuse isn't about being smart enough or having a high IQ (that's an ego-based excuse); it's a belief that information is either beyond your grasp or not worth grasping. Knowledge excuses can prevent you from discovering new things about yourself, your industry, colleagues, employees, and competitors. The kinds of excuses I refer to here are not about intelligence. Rather, they refer to a lack of expansion of your skills, ability, and desire to learn. It's about stretching yourself to do new things, and to dig deeply into those areas that can enrich your life and your understanding of your profession or an area you want to pursue.

To be good at anything as an individual, you need to be open to learning that which you do not know. The learning starts with you. I did not learn the hospitality business in college. I taught myself by benefiting from every work and managerial experience. Now, because I wanted to learn so badly, I have become the teacher. You must figure out what you don't know as you go along. It's not that you have to wait to start something new before learning everything about it, but learning can and must take place "on the job," in real time, otherwise you'll never get anywhere. You must be open to learning at every moment and accepting that you don't know it all, and, most important, humble enough to accept knowledge from wherever it comes. I learn from my employees every day.

You don't think it's important to know every aspect of your job and the responsibilities it takes to make your business work? How about a guy who owns a taxi. His livelihood depends on the cab, so if he's good at his job, he knows when to change the oil, and if he doesn't know how to do it himself, he makes it his business to learn how. If you own a bar, you'd better know how to make a few cocktails. If you run a clothing store, you'd better know how to fold sweaters even if someone else does it for you. That is an important point: how can you teach your staff, your partners, your family, or anyone how to do things correctly if you don't know how to do them yourself? If you don't know how to send a fax, run a copy machine, or your POS system, I suggest you *rethink that arrogance.*

Expressing a lack of engagement, and the attitude that you are above knowing about certain tasks? That's just being an asshole. It indicates that you have no real passion or love for what you are doing. I'm not saying a bartender has to know how to make a hock cobbler without looking it up—but he should know how to make a screwdriver. In short, you should understand the basic components of your job and industry, and learn more about it every day. I emphasize constant improvement because it keeps us on our toes. It's a mind-set that forces us to be conscious of what is going on around us, which in turn opens us up to exciting new ideas.

I understand that some of you might be resistant to the idea of constant learning. You may think that if you learn something once, you don't have to learn it again. That's not exactly true. Consider the story of e-commerce giant Alibaba founder Jack Ma.[1] At the age of twelve, Ma would wake up at five a.m. to walk or ride his bike to the main hotel in his city, Hangzhou, China, so he could practice the English he was learning in school with English-speaking tourists. He did this for nine straight years, also offering his services as a free tour guide to these visitors.

Ma realized that what he was learning in school was not the same as what he was learning from the foreigners he interacted with at the hotel. Sometimes what you are learning might not be the only way to know about something—and it might not even be true in the first place. The skills Ma gained by talking to native English speakers went a long way toward helping him learn about the world. They provided the basis for this poor Chinese kid, who could not even get hired at his local branch of KFC, to start a company that has helped him create a net worth of $21.9 billion—yes, that's *billion* with a *b*.

Constant learning is not only about refreshing what you know. It's very much about deepening understanding, making connections to form new ideas, and building your expertise. No one knows too much. I know a hell of a lot about the bar business—honestly, more overall knowledge than anyone I've ever met—but I would never say that there's nothing left for me to know or learn. I am constantly learning about the television business. Each season I shoot, I learn more about production values and quality storytelling. I also make it a point to keep up with the changing technology in the hospitality business, and learn as much as I can about how it helps bars and restaurants operate more efficiently and profitably.

Increasing your knowledge is available anytime anywhere—and it's mostly free! Paula is a smart woman who I long assumed had always been a power broker in her industry. A top salesperson for a large newspaper chain at a time when newspapers made a great

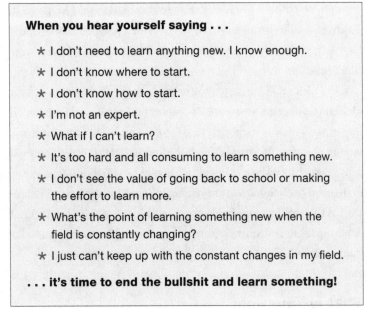

When you hear yourself saying . . .

* ✷ I don't need to learn anything new. I know enough.
* ✷ I don't know where to start.
* ✷ I don't know how to start.
* ✷ I'm not an expert.
* ✷ What if I can't learn?
* ✷ It's too hard and all consuming to learn something new.
* ✷ I don't see the value of going back to school or making the effort to learn more.
* ✷ What's the point of learning something new when the field is constantly changing?
* ✷ I just can't keep up with the constant changes in my field.

. . . it's time to end the bullshit and learn something!

deal of money from ad sales, Paula traveled the country making huge advertising deals with major companies and ran a department of forty salespeople. I had also thought Paula's career trajectory was conventional—from high school to college to work. Wrong. It turns out Paula did not even go to college until she was thirty.

"I thought I was too dumb to go to college, so after high school I got a no-skills-necessary job in retail," she says. Paula worked her way up through the ranks of a large department store for fifteen years. It was at that store where Frank, a manager, noticed that Paula was sharp and capable. "He said to me, 'Paula, you should go to college. You could really advance further in the store with a degree.' I thought he was crazy. I told him I wasn't smart enough for college. My family had told me that and I believed it. Taking an admissions exam or the SAT just seemed like it would be a waste of time and energy. I would fail and just feel even more like a jerk."

Frank kept at Paula, urging her to take the admissions test for Queens College in New York. "I respected Frank, and I figured, if he thinks I'm smart enough to go to college, maybe my family is wrong. *Maybe I'm wrong.*" To her surprise, Paula aced the test, and at age thirty, the mother of two boys, she started college, going on to earn bachelor's degrees in English and business administration. After graduating, Paula accepted a job as a sales manager at a newspaper, and quickly moved up the ranks to run its sales department.

That *Is* Your Job!

One way people avoid learning is by thinking that some tasks at work are not their job—the sort of people who live and die by their job descriptions. This is a popular sentiment because some of us, particularly those who are members of the rank and file, or lower-level staff members, may feel that doing something outside of a job description means they are being taken advantage of, or being asked to work more for less money. This could be true in some instances, and if you go out of your way above and beyond for a long period of time without recognition, it's probably time to look for a new job. However, I think this happens less often than people imagine. Then there are the people who think some jobs are beneath them. When I rescued Jazz Katz in Michigan, I met one chef who refused to wash up because he said he wasn't a dishwasher! That's a big deal when the food you cook, food you're supposed to take pride in, is put on plates that have evidence of mold and grease.

Ironically, people who think narrowly about their responsibilities tend to stay in rank-and-file jobs, while those who want to embrace tasks outside of their job descriptions have greater access to better opportunities and money.

More often, constantly sending the message that you won't do something because it's not your job sends a red flag (in some cases, a black flag!) to those around you, including your bosses and customers. Avoiding any responsibility that is not yours wears you down, and your own aspirations can diminish. If you never step out of your defined role, you never get a chance to interact with different people, ideas, and processes. To the person who says, "That's not my job," I would ask, You have no desire to solve a problem or improve yourself with knowledge outside the minimum required to do your job, so you have no interest in advancing your career? I've always called these types of people skids because they skid through life, never growing, never learning, never being an example, never becoming leaders or special. Do you want to advance, do you want to improve yourself and grow your knowledge? Ask yourself, can I learn from this, can I benefit from it and advance myself? What if your assistant gets sick and his or her replacement is incompetent? What if you're working late and no one is around? You think the janitor is going to get you a cup of coffee? Think again. You have to make your own coffee, buddy. Being uninvolved and not knowledgeable has serious consequences. How can you run the business if you are not involved and engaged? How can you grow, improve your life, and become an example for your friends and family when your chances to grow pass with the moments?

Why do you want to run a business or work in an industry if you do not want to be involved in its very core? You say you simply want to own a business but not run it? I say owners have to understand their businesses so that they can take them to their potential in today's changing market forces and trends.

I worked with a fellow who owned a restaurant for ten years. One day I stopped by and opened the kitchen's large refrigerator. All sorts of items were rotten or rotting: produce, meat, and dairy. It was disgusting. I said to him, What if one of your investors saw this? When was the last time your checked your own kitchen? He told me he hadn't looked in the fridge or the kitchen in years. How could that be? His answer: "I leave kitchen management and ordering to my chef." Food is the second-highest cost center of a restaurant (labor is first). Think about it. Any owner who does not understand the practices and results of his highest cost center is either lazy or a fool.

Learning for Longevity and Success

In a study of 356 U.S. companies between 2000 and 2010, Professor Xueming Luo of the University of Texas measured the value and volatility of stock returns and the strength of relationships between employees and customers.[2] He discovered that the average shelf life of positive performance for executives is about five years. He also found that the longer an executive or manager stays with a company, the further the relationship with her customers declines. As a CEO becomes more established and comfortable, she relies on colleagues and managers for insight, instead of continuing to learn directly from customers. What I take from this research is that for anyone to succeed over the long term, knowledge must be direct—we can't depend on others' interpretations of what's going on in our business.

You may not be the CEO of a large company, but you *are* the CEO of your own life. No matter what role you have in your industry—whether you are a boss, a middle manager, or just starting out—learn to listen, go to the source, and dig deeply to understand what information is true and what is not true. In my experience, the other reason why performance declines over the years is that people—bosses, entrepreneurs, and workers alike—tend to become fixed in their thinking. According to my interpretation of Carol S. Dweck's book *Mindset,* openness to learning begins with developing a "growth" mind-set as opposed to a "fixed" mind-set.[3] A growth mind-set is one that is open to the new and unknown and a fixed mind-set is one that assumes we have a certain amount of intelligence and it cannot be increased. This is all in your head—you're in control over whether you will be growth oriented or set in your ways. Here are ten ways to develop a growth mind-set:

1. Practice active curiosity. Question more.
2. Embrace challenges.
3. Listen and learn from criticism.
4. Don't lose your connection to your customers or stakeholders. Get rid of the middleman, and go directly to the source for information.
5. Try to learn something new every week.
6. Keep yourself fresh and avoid getting too comfortable by seeking out opinions and knowledge from new sources.
7. Always ask yourself if what you believe about your business is really true.

8. Don't automatically accept conventional wisdom.

9. Don't accept anything at face value. Dig deeper.

10. Change your scenery. Take a different route to work. Travel to a new place. Shake up your perspective.

Don't Wait Until You Know Everything to Start (Because You're Never Going to Know Everything)

Too often we let our uncertainties about whether we have what it takes to succeed run our lives. As a result, we tend to avoid new challenges or decline to pursue exciting opportunities that could take us to new levels of personal or professional success and happiness. All because we don't trust our own ability to rise to the challenges that are involved. Remember: effort leads to mastery!

You've definitely been smart enough to accomplish something that was initially scary to you—whether that was starting a new job, writing a plan for a brand-new business, taking a risk by asking for a raise, taking a class to learn a new skill—or doing anything you've never tried before. Don't think for a second that you're not smart enough to make a needed change again. Figure out what it is you need to know to move forward and then find a way to acquire the knowledge.

Don't underestimate your abilities and buy into self-doubt. When you see a gap in your understanding, it's an opportunity to grow and expand. Not doing so is really about fear—the fear of looking like a jerk, the fear of screwing up, the fear of being ashamed and embarrassed. None of it is true. One way of figuring out where you have knowledge gaps is through active self-teaching. My first bar job was at a Colorado steakhouse when I was studying anthropology at the University of Denver. I didn't know how to make the drinks customers ordered. There was no Internet, no Google. I had to learn from my customers—I had to learn how to make the drinks while I was making them. It was clear to me what I knew and what I didn't know.

When I became a consultant in the hospitality business, people would pay me to do a study and a business plan for a restaurant, bar, entertainment venue, or hotel. While I knew a lot about hotels and bars, being a consultant was a different role and I was now in an advisory capacity. I was not their boss, so they were not forced to listen to me. Instead, I had to be prepared to prove everything I recommended and establish my credibility every week. To make certain my work was bulletproof and thorough, I wrote a thirty- to forty-page study for each client to make sure everything was fully conceived and detailed. (Now, more than thirty years later, I still do the same detailed document for every client, and my Taffer Dynamics Market Studies and Business Growth Plans are renowned industry standards.)

That meant I had to learn demographics and psychographics— the study of consumer behavior, personality, values, opinions, attitudes, interests, and lifestyles. I learned how to develop competitive assessments and marketing instructions. It was incredibly eye-opening and valuable information, especially as I continued to grow as a hospitality consultant. I never chose to learn any of these things. It happened because I took on bigger responsibilities and was willing to learn what I didn't know as I went along. I didn't wait to learn about psychographics before becoming a consultant; I was willing to fly without landing gear.

When I took a job at the famed (but now defunct) all-seasons, full-service resort Grossinger's in the early 1980s, I didn't have any experience running a 2,600-seat dining room in an American plan hotel. That means customers pay a single daily rate that covers their room and all their (unlimited) meals—breakfast, lunch, and dinner. Therefore, the dining room was very busy. In addition, Grossinger's was kosher, so I had separate meat and dairy kitchens, with rabbis running around inspecting everything we did. I didn't know anything about resort hotels, convention centers, hosting religious events, headliner entertainment and shows, ski lodges, kosher kitchens, eighteen-hole golf courses and clubhouses, swimming pools, outside catering, or being the manager on duty of a 1,700-room, 1,200-acre property.

I was interviewed at the resort by Mark Grossinger Etess. Mark was a superstar with great presence. Even so, somehow I convinced him (and myself) that I could do it and was hired as the highest nonfamily executive at the property. I did do it and became quite close to the family during those years. The Grossinger family, particularly Elaine and Mark Grossinger Etess, were huge influences on my career. Mark later became Donald Trump's vice president in Atlantic City, where he led the development of Trump's Taj Mahal hotel. Unfortunately, years later, Mark was killed with several other executives when Trump's helicopter crashed on the Garden State Parkway.

Being entrepreneurial, I knew I could learn on the job and adapt to what was happening at any given moment. Agility is crucial when you learn while doing. I took risks and made it my personal responsibility to figure out how to deliver on my promise to run the resort properly. I managed to maintain my credibility without showing ignorance. I asked the right questions, I listened, I didn't show weakness, and I didn't talk about things I didn't know about. Because of all this, the family and the department heads respected me, supported me, and helped me learn what I didn't know.

During a consulting job, I met a woman I'll call Carol, who was a managing partner at one of the nation's top consulting firms. Carol told me she had declined offers to take on a senior leadership role in her firm for years. She told herself that she just did not have the capacity, skills, or knowledge to succeed and that if she took the new role, she would embarrass herself and become a disappointment to her boss and her colleagues. Fortunately, her boss knew she had the ability to do the job well and so he offered her the job over and over until she finally—and hesitatingly—accepted.

After she accepted the job, Carol sat down and analyzed the requirements of the role. She then made two lists: one of the things she already knew how to do and the other of the things she would have to learn. The leadership at her company, who believed in her potential, set her up in training programs. A senior executive mentored her for the first few months on the job. Carol also did job-related reading and research at night, and sought the advice of people who were already doing the job. She took a couple of courses, which the company was happy to pay for, to augment what she learned on the job and from her own studying. In retrospect, Carol said, she had believed her own lies about her abilities, but was able to overcome them when she stopped making excuses about her ability to add to her knowledge base.

If you truly think you are not "good enough" to do something that seems more difficult than what you are comfortably doing now, ask yourself what it is you think you don't know. We all have the capacity to learn new things and to master new skills. If you really don't know something, figure out who or what can teach you what you need to know.

A friend of mine recently told me a story about her niece. The seventeen-year-old applied for an entry-level service job at Panera, the popular soup and sandwich place. She had a group interview with four other candidates of similar age and education. None had previous work experience, so the playing field was level. The interviewer asked each candidate why he or she wanted to work at Panera. My friend's niece replied, "I like the food here; it's great quality. And I think for that reason it would be a great place to work." Well, okay, it's a reason, but it's not the best one she could have come up with.

Another candidate had clearly done a little research online before the interview. He explained that he respected the restaurant's "food as it should be" mission and how it sought out the freshest ingredients. He talked about the history of the company and its philosophy, and expressed admiration for those principles. He told the interviewer that he wanted to learn more about how the company followed through on its promise to customers, and was looking forward to learning how he could contribute to that promise.

No surprise, the boy got the job. The information he included in his answer is available on the company Web site. No magic, no nepotism, no discrimination—just a bit of learning. It made all the difference for him in getting the job over the other candidates. It's shocking how many people don't put forth even this small effort. I know because I've been on the other side of the table, interviewing people who didn't know the most basic information about working behind a bar or taking an order from a customer. Honestly, that's just being lazy. In my job interviews, I always ask the candidate about my business, our specialties, and what we do. If they did not take the time to learn anything about the company, they do not have the discipline or desire to work for it, and therefore for me.

Access What's Available and Devote the Right Resources to Learning

So many resources exist, from online courses to old-fashioned night school, mentoring opportunities, and training programs. There is no reason you can't learn new things anytime and at any age. Learning can be as simple as finding someone whom you admire and studying how they do things. The motivational speaker Tony Robbins says that the greatest way to find success is to learn and mimic a successful person. If you want to be a great financier, study Warren Buffett. If you want to be an amazing tennis player, practice and analyze Serena and Venus Williams's techniques. The people who teach you don't even have to be alive. I am inspired by Thomas Jefferson's ability to develop relationships and bring people together rather than pull them apart. Billionaire aviator, film producer, and business tycoon Howard Hughes had the ability to provide a vision, then delegate it and execute it through a team. I admire and learn from that.

Massive open online courses, or MOOCs, have made all sorts of information easily accessible. From YouTube videos that tell you how to do everything from rewiring a lamp to restoring a vintage car to online courses at Ivy League colleges like Stanford on subjects as diverse as constitutional law and children's nutrition, there's no reason continuous learning can't be a part of your everyday life. If you think you don't want to learn about a subject because you didn't enjoy school or weren't good at it, remember that now you are choosing subjects that interest you. What are you curious about? If you are interested in a subject, learning about it is going to be a pleasure. Teaching has also evolved and become more dynamic and experiential. Find teachers who inspire you. They're out there. Here are just a few of the ever-expanding resources available:

* iTunes U, a section of Apple's iTunes music store, is dedicated to providing educational audio and video files from universities, museums, and media organizations. Participating institutions include Stanford, UC Berkeley, University of Melbourne, Texas A&M, MIT, Yale, and Trinity College Dublin. The Beyond Campus section of iTunes U provides free educational content from American Public Media, PBS, the Museum of Modern Art, and the Smithsonian.

* The Khan Academy offers free practice exercises and instructional videos in math, science, computer programming, history, art history, economics, and other subjects. Khan has partnered with institutions like NASA, the Museum of Modern Art, the California Academy of Sciences, and MIT to offer specialized content.

* The OEDb (Open Education Database) is the most comprehensive collection of online free courses anywhere. It features more than ten thousand free open courses and interactive resources from top universities around the world.

* Harvard Extension School features free online education courses from Harvard University.

* Open Yale Courses, UC Berkeley Class Central, MIT Open-CourseWare, Carnegie Mellon Open Learning Initiative, University of London podcasts, and University of Oxford podcasts

are all offered for free. Imagine getting an Ivy League–level education at your own pace, from home or anywhere, *for free!*

There are dozens of other free Web sites that offer similar course work on just about any subject you can think of, including Coursera, Open Culture online courses, Udemy, Academic Earth, edX, Alison, Codecademy, SCORE, and many more—and there are new resources added to the Internet all the time.

There are also many low-cost learning organizations, institutions, and opportunities available out there. Getting certifications in your profession can be an important investment if they help you earn certain levels of achievement and credibility. If passing a real estate test and getting your real estate license means you can start your own agency and make more money, what are you waiting for? It amazes me that there are people who are willing to travel hundreds and sometimes thousands of miles to attend a conference to see me in person but are more hesitant to make a small investment that requires no travel to learn from TVT (Taffer Virtual Teaching), my on-demand learning tool with more than sixty on-demand online lessons for hospitality industry owners, managers, and service staff; complete testing; and Taffer certifications.

Nearly every industry offers similar on-demand virtual teaching programs. These are great investments because they let you work at your own speed and conform them to your schedule. Plus most educational programs are tax deductible. If a master's degree or a professional degree like an MBA will help you get a better job, it's worth the time and money to get it, especially because you can do that from home now too.

There is absolutely no reason why you cannot expand your expertise, learn new skills, and improve your business chops, even if you work full time.

Here are my top tips for becoming a continuous learner:

1. Own what you don't know, and make it a point to educate yourself. Don't assume you know enough to continue to grow and succeed. You don't.

2. Make a list of what you need to know to evolve your career or your life. Try to check one of those things off the list once a month. Review and update it monthly.

3. Find someone you admire and learn how he became a success. Do what he does. It doesn't matter whether you know him or not—we can learn about how famous people have become successful without ever standing next to them.

4. Before meeting someone important to your business or going on a job interview, do your homework. Understand the background and mission of the person or business, and learn what questions to ask.

5. Devote at least fifteen minutes a day to learning something new and continuing your education. For instance, read a chapter of a book on a subject you are learning to master, read articles, or listen to a podcast. Practice your skills—take the time to perfect making two new cocktails if you work in a bar, or practice the guitar if that is your passion. Whatever you are pursuing, you can carve out fifteen minutes a day to do it.

Learn from Those You Serve

Learning from your customers is vital to your success. Even if you work in a back office or don't deal directly with the public, you are serving someone in your job. You have a boss—and the boss is really your customer, right? You have to think of the people you work for (and if you have a job, you work for someone) as customers. Doing so gives you greater buy-in to the idea that your job is part of a bigger universe—it's not just you toiling away on a computer making sure the numbers add up (or whatever it is you do). Someone, somewhere, is counting on you to hold up your end of the bargain and to do your job better, and you can learn from that person (or people).

Customers, whatever form they take, are not unchanging automatons who continue to behave the same way year after year. That is particularly true today, when social media, information connectedness, and greater mobility offer nearly limitless options for how people shop, consume, and spend time. It's your job to keep up with your consumers, and to continuously learn from them, so you can keep your core, add new customers, and lure back once-loyal defectors.

When Elizabeth DeRose wrote to J.Crew to complain about their latest line of clothing, which she felt had veered too far from the company's classic and timeless style, she had no idea that its CEO, Millard "Mickey" Drexler, would read the note personally and then pick up the phone to call her. Elizabeth's husband, Chris DeRose, coauthor of *Judgment on the Front Line: How Smart Companies Win by Trusting Their People,* gives an account of the interaction in *Forbes.*[4] Apparently, Elizabeth's e-mail about the company's 2013 collection prompted Drexler to respond to her criticism in fewer than twenty-four hours. How many CEOs do you know who do this?

J.Crew's leadership asked Chris's wife what she liked and didn't like about the company's new vision and listened. Drexler also defended his commitment to continually evolve the brand, but admitted that some recent choices might have strayed too far from J.Crew's timeless style, which had alienated many long-standing customers. Drexler noted that he had visited J.Crew retail stores and could sense customers' dissatisfaction with some of the new styles. "We are on it for sure," he later e-mailed Chris's wife. "I hope you see a difference this fall."

Understanding what customers want provides a frontline education—and gives you insights that show up on a P&L (profit and loss) statement later, when it could be too late. We don't like to connect falling profits to customer reactions, but they are intimately connected. J.Crew's pursuit of customer feedback is remarkable because so few companies, large and small alike, do it. We may talk about customer feedback, but how many of us really act on it?

ENGAGE ON SOCIAL MEDIA

If you don't regularly monitor your own social media pages for customer research and reactions, start now. It's amazing to me that so many insightful and rich conversations take place on social media pages, and owners either ignore them or don't take them seriously as an indication of how people feel about their businesses. Comments, conversation threads, shares, likes, and retweets show you what people are thinking about and what is really important to them. You might be going in the wrong direction while the right one is blazing across the Internet, only you're too stubborn or distracted to notice. Customer conversations can also tell you if your branding strategies are working—are customers "getting it" or missing the point? If they are missing the point, that's your problem, not theirs.

There is an independent Web site called BarRescueUpdates .com that I believe was originally created to beat the hell out of my rescues because the people who started the site expected them to fail. At the end of the day, 70 percent or more of our rescues succeed, so it was hard for the writers to be negative. The site became reasonably fair and I find it an interesting place for information about my audience. Fans chat and say how they feel. I'm on Twitter during almost every episode of *Bar Rescue* (when I'm not taping or traveling). Being there to hear my audience's reaction to me and my work is very important to me. As a professional who always wants to do better, I can't imagine not seeking out and considering audience opinions and feedback. What people say and how they feel are very important to me.

Paying regular attention to review sites like TripAdvisor and Yelp and to comments on your Facebook and Twitter accounts should be a regular part of your learning. Forums, Reddit, and LinkedIn groups are also potential resources for customer information. Your customers dwell in these places, and the level of discourse and discussion found there is often detailed and informative. Tools such as the free service Social Mention helps you track conversations about your brand that are happening in real time. Google Alerts also helps you keep track of mentions of your brand or products.

I believe that you should engage and respond to both critical and praiseful people on social media, or personally if it is possible to reach out to a happy or unhappy customer. It's profitable to do so. It's also proper courtesy. A survey of more than three thousand consumers done by consulting firm Bain found that people who engage with companies on social media spend 20 to 40 percent more money with those companies than people who don't interact.[5] When you see social media comments from people about your business, they are most likely from paying customers—don't throw away the chance (and money) to learn from them and make them happy!

However, you have to be careful when talking online to customers. Canned responses on social media and review sites don't fool anyone and are, in fact, insulting. For instance, on the popular travel Web site TripAdvisor, when someone leaves a negative review, some establishments, whether a restaurant, hotel, or recreational facility, leave obvious auto responses.

For instance, a large hotel chain leaves this response every time they receive a one-star review on TripAdvisor:

On behalf of our entire team, I would like to apologize for not exceeding your expectations. Your satisfaction is important to us and we will be using the feedback you gave us to implement improvements to ensure we offer a better experience for guests in the future. I hope that you will consider staying with us again so that we can have another chance to provide you with a superior experience. If I can provide any assistance, please don't hesitate to contact me directly at [phone number].

Sincerely,
[general manager's name]

How did I know it was canned? First, the same exact message was left for every one-star review. Further, one person left a very positive review, but gave the review itself only one star (probably a typo), and the reviewer received the same reply from the hotel. That's a sign that the hotel has a system that automatically leaves that response for any one-star review, regardless of what the review itself actually says. None of the responses dealt with any of the varied and specific complaints in the comments. Readers are left feeling as if the actual issues were not being dealt with; it's just lip service. In this sense, disingenuous, generic responses can be more destructive than not responding at all, because people don't believe them.

If you are going to respond to critical remarks, do so graciously and with replies that refer to the specific issues customers describe. Let them know what you are going to do about it, and offer to discuss the problem with the customer personally. Respond to positive comments in the same individual fashion. Other readers notice how you respond to both critics and fans—and this does contribute to the overall impression they have of your business. According to research done by American Express, 70 percent of Americans are willing to spend an average of 13 percent more with companies they believe provide excellent customer service.[6] Any interaction with customers online should demonstrate an authentic interest in resolving problems and providing great experiences.

OBSERVE AND LISTEN

A fancy name for watching your customers and interpreting their behavior is ethnographic research. You may not have the kind of budget required to hire an anthropologist to report back from "the field," but there is no reason why you can't do what J.Crew CEO Mickey Drexler does. If you have a physical location with customers, mingle with them, watch, listen, and engage. Listen to what they say, and notice how they react to and interact with your product.

Observation and curiosity made me a successful hotel manager in the 1980s, before I started my consulting business. Every day I walked my properties, filling the coffee cups in the dining room and asking how customers' stays were going. I had to be belly to belly, look in their eyes, and feel how they felt. I wanted to see their faces when they ate the food. Comment cards served a purpose, but only a small percentage of people filled them out and what they said generally represented extremes both negative and positive. If there was a problem, for example, if a patron didn't like the steak, I would say, "No problem, let's get you another steak." I would bring it to him myself, and then circle back later to find out if the second steak was satisfactory. This is not just a chance to right something wrong but a chance to connect. Face-to-face interaction gives you a richer, more meaningful, and more accurate picture of how customers feel about your business. Don't miss out on the opportunity to connect directly with people and learn from them.

It is not just the guests I was interested in. I wanted to know how my employees felt too. Sure, I could hear it from my department managers, but I knew they were not giving me a full, accurate picture. It's not because they were deceptive or trying to hide things from me (although some were). They were giving me their points of view, and because I was the boss, they always wanted to put a positive spin on things. I would run the dish machine with the dishwasher or stand with the line cook while he chopped tomatoes. I saw this as an opportunity to connect with the team. When they were slammed I helped them. I'd grab a broom and sweep the floors with them. As I did these things, we talked in a setting that was familiar and comfortable for them, and I was able to gather a great deal of information about how they felt about the way the kitchen was being run.

I would have lunch with the housekeeping staff every week. There would be thirty or forty housekeepers and me. It was the best way to find out where the carpets were wearing out, or if the furniture needed to be replaced. Housekeeping staff members in hotels are under constant pressure to perform (so next time you get good service, acknowledge it! Housekeeping staff work very hard). In the hotels I managed we expected housekeepers to turn over a room in eighteen minutes, which is not unusual. It was imperative that I knew what the problems were because problems cost time. Using the wrong chemicals, not having the proper tools, running out of supplies, improperly set up maids' carts—all of these missteps cost time. If we could figure out how to drive the time down to sixteen minutes per room, even better. If I wanted my staff to want to drive down their turnover time, I had to connect with them regularly. They had to know I cared, respected what they did, and provided the tools they needed to be successful. How would I accomplish anything as a manager if I didn't sit with them and achieve it with them?

ASK QUESTIONS

If you don't have a physical location, find other ways to interact. J.Crew's Drexler called customers, something you can do too, if and when appropriate. What would happen if you called five dissatisfied customers each month? What problems would you learn about and solve? On the flip side, what if you also called five happy customers and learned about why they like the business and what keeps them coming back? Imagine the wealth of material you could get from just five people—perhaps more insights and ideas than an entire crew of Ph.D.'s in anthropology could come up with after a year in the field. Better yet, it wouldn't cost you a dime.

You can also use surveys and questionnaires to get insights into the feelings, needs, desires, and behaviors of customers as an alternative to firsthand observation. Anonymous surveys may produce more honest responses than those in which the person is identified. When designing a survey, keep questions specific and geared toward getting the information you want to know. Don't waste your customers' time; keep the survey as short as possible while still making it enjoyable, useful, and pertinent. Sites like SurveyMonkey allow you to design surveys to measure customer feelings, measure benchmarks, and gather material about consumer habits. Years ago, I conducted a satisfaction survey with customers. At the same time, I conducted an employee survey asking them what they thought customer opinions were. The disconnect was incredible. My employees believed one thing and my customers believed another. Listening to your employees is helpful. Listening to your customers is everything.

Expanding your learning via asking questions isn't something you can do only with customers—you can ask questions of your managers, people who report to you, your colleagues, your friends, and your family.

Bullshit Buster: Larry Ruvo

Larry Ruvo, cofounder, chairman, and senior managing director of Southern Glazer's Wine and Spirits of Nevada, has been a part of the wine and spirits distribution business in Las Vegas since 1970. He spent the early part of his professional life working at the Venetian Restaurant (owned by his parents) and managing the Los Angeles Playboy Club, as well stints at the Sahara Hotel, Caesars Palace, and the Frontier Hotel before starting a liquor distributorship with Steve Wynn. That business eventually grew into the distributor Southern Wine and Spirits of Nevada and is now called Southern Glazer's Wine and Spirits of Nevada.

Larry also established UNLVino, one of the largest annual wine-tasting events in the country. In addition to his business leadership, he's also well known in the Las Vegas community for his philanthropy, particularly his dedication to finding a cure for Alzheimer's disease, something his father suffered from. Larry is also chairman and cofounder of Keep Memory Alive and the Cleveland Clinic Lou Ruvo Center for Brain Health, for which he devotes his time and energy to finding a cure for Alzheimer's and other neurodegenerative diseases.

I have so much respect for Larry. In my forty years in the hospitality business, there are very few people who have affected me as profoundly as he has, and in such a short time. I met Larry about a year ago, and the love and affection I have for him now is immense. He has inspired me as a businessperson and a philanthropist. He is my role model. Larry excels in his personal life, touching so many with his commitment to helping people and his community virtually every day. Larry and his organization support more than three hundred charitable causes each year. His commitment to helping those in need is greater than anyone I've met. Because of Larry, I have been moved to contribute to Keep Memory Alive and to become involved as a member of the board of trustees of St. Jude's Ranch for Children, all because of my desire to emulate his goodness.

Larry has taught me a great deal and I respect his wisdom. He learned early on that it is unwise to be too confident about what you know and don't know—and that one's education never ends.

Larry grew up working at his parents' Italian restaurant in Las Vegas. As a kid he did a variety of things there—grated cheese, washed pans, bused tables. By the time he was a teen, he thought he knew everything about the restaurant. So when a chef who Larry thought had been drinking argued with him, he took matters into his own hands and fired him. Larry was fourteen at the time.

The decision wasn't very popular with the actual owners—Mom and Dad—Larry recalls. "My father came to work and said, 'I understand you fired the chef. Never fire a chef on a Friday, Larry. We need him for the weekend, so hire him back.' We sat down at this tiny table and I told John I had made a mistake and I needed to bring him back. I apologized and told him I had acted too quickly (knowing he would be fired on Monday... so I thought). My father said to him, 'John, you are hired back *and* you are now promoted to general manager. Now I want you to fire my son.'"

Larry's father taught him an important lesson about not knowing everything—and that there was a price to pay for the arrogance of thinking you did. "It was a big moment in my life," Larry says.

After that incident, Larry never worked for his father again. Instead, he went to work as a busboy at the Sahara on the Las Vegas

Strip, and found other jobs as he developed and learned about the hospitality business. He never forgot the lesson his father had taught him, and even today he applies it to his successful distributorship. It's a lesson he makes sure is instilled in all the people who work with and for him at Southern Glazer's Wine and Spirits.

"I don't believe one person has the ability to do hiring," he says. "Multiple people do an interview; it's a team that we put together so we can gather a variety of opinions. They see things I may not see and vice versa."

Larry puts an emphasis on all of his employees being people who are open to learning because, as he says, turnover is expensive and he wants his businesses to be places to learn and share. The openness also helps people become smarter managers and businesspeople in the end. "Inexperienced managers like I was [at fourteen] do a lot of damage," he said. "That's why no one has the authority to fire a person on the spot. We have to know it's not emotional; it's not personality. There has to be a legitimate work-related reason to let someone go. We want to make sure of that."

Larry also learned a key lesson about not making excuses about learning. He was the only child in a family that had very little money, and he had to figure out how to do things on his own. "My father always told me, 'When your mom and I are gone, who will be there if you cannot pay the rent? No one. If something breaks, learn how to fix it yourself because if you wait for a mechanic to come they may not show up.' That's how I have lived my life. You need to get that rent check together yourself; you have to learn to repair what's broken," Larry says.

That learning comes in part from asking questions. If Larry had asked his father about the chef before firing him, he might not have been released from the family business at such a young age.

Now Larry makes sure his own employees know that asking questions is not frowned upon, but rather the way you take control of your own destiny. "We provide a great amount of resources for our people to be successful, so if they fail it's because they didn't ask questions," Larry says of his company. "Ask questions, ask for help. If I don't know the answer, I'll find the answer. But you have to ask the question first. Too often people are embarrassed to raise their hands—and those are the people who are no longer with us or no longer successful."

Bullshit Buster: Jim Zumpone

In the northeast corner of Pennsylvania, in the tiny hamlet of Lakeville, sits a factory: Supreme Zipper Industries, a full-service zipper manufacturer and supply company. When owner and CEO Jim Zumpone became involved in the zipper business in 2001, it was dying, as were other manufacturing industries in the United States. Jim was thirty-one and just coming to terms with the fact that his passion for carpentry would not sustain him long term, as back problems made it next to impossible for him to continue to build things. He had to find something else to do—something that would hold his interest *and* support his growing family. One day, while at an appointment with his optometrist, the conversation turned to his life situation. Dr. Rozenberg, whom knew Jim well, suggested he meet with his father, Sol, who owned a zipper company.

Jim had nothing to lose, so he went up to a tiny loft on Twenty-eighth Street in New York City to meet Sol, a wisp of a man wearing a beautiful suit, custom shirt, and cuff links. "Sol had been Supreme Zipper's sole proprietor since 1950. The company had gone from several hundred employees in the 1960s to a one-hundred-year-old man in an eight-hundred-square-foot loft buying and selling zippers in 2001," Jim recalls.

The zipper industry was highly segmented at this point as well. Some zipper companies made only zippers for garments, others made industrial zippers, or zippers for furniture, and so on. No factory was making zippers for all industries. Jim thought that he could revive the business by becoming a one-stop shop for zipper needs across users—but to change the industry and the way things had been done for years, he needed to learn, and fast.

"I had to understand the furniture trade, the boat-cover business, garment making, industrial-zipper needs, everything," Jim says. "It was a huge learning curve, particularly since I had been a carpenter and not a manufacturer." If he was going to grow the business and teach other people how to do this as well, it needed to start with him. Jim did know how to build things and was mechanically minded. How different could building a staircase be from creating a zipper? There was only one way to find out.

He started his learning from scratch, by first learning how to make a simple zipper. He took it apart and put it back together again. He asked Sol about zipper making, and studied zippers in all their variations. There was and is no Zipper University—so teaching himself was the only choice.

Continuous learning is a hallmark of the company. Today, if Supreme doesn't make a zipper, or if someone comes to them with a need that has never been filled, Jim figures out a way to get it made, even if it means developing it from scratch, which can take a lot of trial and error. In order for this to work, Jim says, he's made sure everyone in his company knows that they have the freedom to make mistakes while trying to learn something new and solve a problem—and that they won't be penalized for trying.

"I don't like my employees to be afraid to tell me there was a mistake. I don't place blame unless it is something blatant," Jim says. "Instead, I ask, how can we go forward so we avoid this problem?" He also makes it a point to tell employees that solving problems is a group responsibility—everyone should be paying attention to the final product.

"It's amazing how many nuances we have ironed out by giving every person the ability to stop everything if they see something wrong," he says. "It's important for the employees to know that because once we hand off a shipment to UPS, we have no way to fix it. We try to be perfect when it goes out the door. I don't care if the last person before the truck comes is the one who says something is wrong, we have to unpack the boxes and fix it. But I want my people to feel that I will solve the problem with them. Usually the same problem does not happen again."

Because Supreme has a culture of continuous learning, Jim can handle oddball requests that many of his competitors cannot. One customer came to him with a request for a one-hundred-foot-long zipper made of heavy-gauge plastic that would be used to protect expensive helicopter cables. Another asked him to make a zipper that was water resistant on both sides. Although these projects weren't part of their bread and butter, Jim and his staff were willing to put in the work to tackle new products and accommodate their customers. This kind of attention and willingness to experiment and learn has helped Supreme stay ahead of its competitors, including those in China, and stay relevant in a business that's harder to succeed in today.

Jim attributes the "whatever it takes" attitude to a lesson he learned in his youth. "When I was sixteen I teamed up with an older cousin who was in his forties in the carpentry business," he says. "He taught me about POTJ—part of the job. It doesn't matter if you are the carpenter, if you make a mess, clean it up. Do what you need to do to make the business work. At Supreme, it was rough in the beginning for people who didn't understand that idea, but I think you learn more and you remain on top of things when you are willing to do whatever is necessary."

Bullshit Buster: Maria Menounos

New England native Maria Menounos is an Emmy-winning journalist, an actress, a television host, an author, a part-time professional wrestler, an entrepreneur, and an industry disruptor. Maria has had an amazing career trajectory, due to her own persistence, willingness to learn, tenacity for constant improvement, and enthusiasm for trying new things. Not bad for a kid from a lower-middle-class background with no connections in the TV world. She graduated from Emerson College in Boston in 2000. During her senior year she worked as a reporter for Channel One News. In 2002, she caught the eye of executives at *Entertainment Tonight* and, at just twenty-three years old, became the youngest person ever to host the iconic show. In 2005, she joined NBC to report and host *Access Hollywood*, the *Today Show*, and *Nightly News* while continuing to act. In 2014, Maria signed a multiyear contract with E! to host and produce several programs, including hosting *E! News*. She also hosts *Conversations with Maria*, a daily, top-rated, one-hour radio show on SiriusXM Stars channel and NCM's Noovie, a cinema preshow, seen daily on over 70 percent of America's movie screens. Along with partner Keven Undergaro,

Maria founded and currently serves as the CEO of the AfterBuzz TV Network, a digital broadcast net that produces after shows for favorite TV shows. "I was an outsider to show business and had to learn so much the hard way," she says. "For that reason, I'm super-sensitive to what young people have to endure on the way up and I try to give as many of them the education I didn't have. As sensitive as I am to their plight, I know young people still have to put in the work. They have to make wise choices, be humble, open to training, positive, ever evolving, and resilient. Most of all they have to own up to and accept responsibility for their shortcomings and to never make excuses for when things go awry. That's usually toughest for any of us. It's easy to blame everyone and everything and not ourselves. The latter takes security and courage. However, when you don't embrace excuses, when you instead embrace solutions, you get success—just like Jon says on *Bar Rescue*. That is a success mentality.

"When I started my radio show, we went through a difficult process initially. The woman I hired as my producer, Lauren Lograsso, had told me that radio was her dream. The problem was that Lauren had no experience in the medium. However, I hired her because I believe in hiring for heart over skill—and still do.

"For Lauren's tremendous passion and raw talent, she made her share of mistakes our first year, as any rookie would. At first, there was frustration on both ends and excuses for the errors, but her heart prevailed. In time, Lauren found the courage to admit shortcomings and the strength to hang in. She resolved to create daily solutions. Today, she is literally one of the best producers in all of SiriusXM," says Maria.

When she looks back at her own career, Maria says she wishes more people had pulled her aside and told her what she was doing wrong, because it would have saved pain and suffering and helped her grow. "In our business, people are fearful to tell you the truth and can even be dishonest. It would have been better to hear what mistakes I was making so I could have been given the opportunity to make adjustments. This is why it's important to educate your employees before you dismiss or fire them. Many just need to be exposed to the lessons. The ones with heart will stick around but it's on the employer to teach them." If people aren't giving you the unvarnished reality and constructive feedback, though, it's up to you to go ask for it. "No one would tell me, so I put myself out there and asked for the truth," she says.

Maria and I are close friends who share many personal feelings. I know her heart and really appreciate what she says about teaching and guiding people and learning together. As someone who had never done a television show before, it was a learning process for me when I started working on *Bar Rescue* in 2010 (it debuted on Spike TV in July 2011), just as it was a learning process for Maria when she went into radio.

Even though I knew little about the business of actually making a television show, I knew that *Bar Rescue* was a great idea for a reality program and that I was the right person to do it. I had the personality and the background—I could learn the technical stuff. I had some idea of what to expect, but there were many surprises, and some of my assumptions about making television were challenged.

I depended on the smart television people around me to help me acquire the skills and knowledge to make sure the show expressed the vision I had for it. Early in the show's run, I was co-executive producer because I relied upon the expertise of television professionals over my own. Now, six years and 150 episodes later, I'm the executive producer of *Bar Rescue* and I rarely trust anyone's opinion over mine. But even running my own show, I still never stop learning about ways to improve it, make it more exciting, and maintain viewer engagement.

Every season has seen an increase in our reach and fan base. Approximately 71 million unique viewers have watched season four of *Bar Rescue*. That's about 25 percent of the television universe! People have many choices when deciding how to spend their media time, and I want them to choose my work again and again, so I must keep learning and making it better. People also have choices of where and how they spend their money. If you want your business to keep its core customers happy, and if you want to continually add new business, you can't stop learning. You can't believe you know enough or know it all. Circumstances, demographics, tastes, and trends are continually shifting. If you don't keep up, you'll be left behind.

There are opportunities to learn and expand every day—take them or lose!

DBY To-Do List

* Expand your job whenever possible. Instead of refusing to do something that's not in your job description, jump at the chance to learn a new skill and spend time with people whom you don't see often or at all. Not only will your opportunities for advancement improve (by showing you're willing to pitch in), you can learn all sorts of valuable lessons and gain important insights into your business and people.

* Learn for longevity. You may not be the CEO of a large company, but you *are* the CEO of your own life. No matter what role you play in your industry—whether you are a boss, a middle manager, or just starting out—you're never too advanced or "important" to ask questions, listen, and look for direct sources of information. Continual learning is an investment in your future success.

* Don't wait until you know everything to start. There's never a perfect time to start a new project or business. Start now and learn as you go!

* Access what's available and devote the right resources to learning. There are numerous free and low-cost learning tools online and in your own community. That means there really is no excuse not to acquire skills and knowledge. Time isn't even an excuse, because everyone has at least a few minutes a day that they can use to prioritize learning.

* Learn from those you serve. Pay attention to your constituents and stakeholders, whoever they may be. You can learn a lot from the people who count on you for services and products.

Chapter 3

✳

EXCUSE #3:
TIME

"So what do we do? Anything. Something. So long as we just
don't sit there. If we screw it up, start over. Try something
else. If we wait until we've satisfied all the uncertainties, it
may be too late."

—Lee Iacocca, American automobile executive

Excuses Based on Lack of Time and a
False Sense of Overwhelming Business

I don't have enough time. I am being pulled in too many directions.
Someone or something is stealing my time. Whether you complain that you are overworked and overextended or you believe
that other people, obligations, or competing loyalties are forcing
you to postpone or cancel your own aspirations or dreams, you're
basically saying one thing: you are inefficient. Yes, it's your fault.
It's bullshit and you can change that.

When we talk about equality in life, the one thing that we all have in common and in the same quantity is time. I'll go so far as to say that how we use our time defines our lives. Each day when we awaken, we all have twenty-four hours. We can use those hours wisely or we can make up excuses and use them poorly. Time used well bestows incredible benefits: it helps us make more money, forge important relationships, and break down adversarial ones; it creates camaraderie and allows us to bond with those whom we love and respect; it brings us joy and the chance to experience the world. Time used wisely offers these things and so many more.

Conversely, not appreciating time or understanding its value can lead to life's greatest losses. Not calling my mother for such a long time is an example of how can we fritter away the gift each day gives us. The refusal to reach out to my mother placed a chip on my shoulder—and I sometimes wonder how my life would have been better had I not allowed myself to let that happen. It's very personal, but should serve as a cautionary tale for anyone who is thinking about throwing time away. We cannot get back wasted time.

I see people paralyzed by time wasters like checking e-mail and social media, and bogged down by simple tasks they could easily delegate. The amount of time we devote to social media proves that we have plenty of time for the things we like. No, you're not too busy! Maybe you just need to rethink your priorities.

It's not that you don't have enough time, it's that you are not assessing and valuing your time properly. A 2014 study published in the *Journal of Consumer Research* shows that the natural inclination to categorize time is to put it in "present" and "future" boxes.[1] When we classify a deadline as a future goal, we put in the "someday" file and are more likely to neglect it. Those future time goals may nag at us, but we rarely get them done. When we term something as a "current" responsibility, we're likely to start working on it right away. The problem is that many of the current tasks may be less important than the future tasks in terms of our long-term aspirations. For instance, getting a project done on deadline is important, but plotting out goals you need to reach over the next six months in order to get a promotion and a raise is crucial.

If you have trouble spending your time wisely, you're not alone. Consulting firm McKinsey & Company asked fifteen hundred executives how they spent their time.[2] Only 9 percent of the respondents said they were very satisfied with the way they allocated their time. That's very low. Less than half were somewhat satisfied and a full one-third were actively dissatisfied. Only 52 percent of the respondents said they spent their time in a way that mirrored their companies' strategic goals. Nearly half said they didn't concentrate enough on guiding the strategic direction of the business. If executives feel this way about the way they are spending their time, we can assume that other workers feel similarly. When was the last time you felt incredibly productive, like you absolutely nailed everything on your daily to-do list?

Procrastination Puts You off Your Game

Procrastination is a belief that time is not going to go away. Yet as anyone who has ever missed a cutoff date or been up against an April 15 tax deadline knows, time *is* finite. Moreover, we will die someday. As the great artist Pablo Picasso said, "Only put off until tomorrow what you are willing to die having left undone."

Unfortunately, procrastination feeds on itself. It's an addictive behavior, like smoking or overeating—and, like these negative

When you hear yourself saying . . .

* I'm too busy for that.

* It takes too much time.

* If I do that I won't have time for anything else.

* I have too much to do so nothing gets done.

* Everything takes longer than I think it will.

* I am stuck on how to prioritize.

* Too many people make too many demands on me so I have no room for the things I want to do.

. . . it's time to lose your time excuse and stop bullshitting yourself!

habits, it can have devastating consequences. Just because you feel lazy or uninspired (it happens to all of us) doesn't mean you have to indulge those feelings and give in to them. Okay, so you're not in the mood to revamp your accounting system or tackle some other large project. I doubt you'll feel any more inspired to do it in a week or two, though. If you are procrastinating, ask yourself, is my future important enough to do this, or some of it, today? This question takes you to someplace very deep. Will I move forward or will I stay in my cage?

Procrastination is not just a benign part of human nature. It can be harmful. A friend of mine I'll call Howard was focused on opening a world-class nightclub in Miami. Rather than pushing to get it done quickly, he procrastinated, delayed, and opened six months later than he had planned. The six-month delay not only added rent and other expenses to his budget, he completely missed the Florida winter season. Rather than opening in November to capture it, Howard opened in March, when the winter season was over and the snowbirds had flown up north. He missed his opportunity, lost even more money during the off-season, and closed before the next winter season even began. Two years wasted and millions of dollars lost. Procrastination is completely unacceptable to me. In fact, to be honest, even a moderate pace is not acceptable to me. I'm all about pushing to get it done.

Procrastination has both an emotional and a behavioral factor. We don't want to do something for a variety of reasons, and that translates into avoidance behaviors. Thoughts turn into actions, or inactions in this case. Not doing what we know needs to get done could have a neurological component. Fuschia Sirois of Bishop's University and Timothy Pychyl of Carleton University, both in Canada, found that procrastinators comfort themselves in the present with the false belief that they'll be more emotionally equipped to handle a task in the future.[3] "The future self becomes the beast of burden for procrastination," says Sirois. "We're trying to regulate our current mood and thinking our future self will be in a better state. They'll be better able to handle feelings of insecurity or frustration with the task. That somehow we'll develop these miraculous coping skills to deal with these emotions that we just can't deal with right now."

Pychyl adds, "It's an existentially relevant problem, because [procrastination] is not getting on with life itself. You only get a certain number of years. What are you doing?" Good question.

Your "later" self won't necessarily be more disciplined than your "right now" self. If you let yourself slack off now, you're building a habit of procrastination and actually making it less likely that your later self will get anything done. Accomplishments and achievements do not happen by mistake or by themselves—they are the result of a conscious effort to *take action*. Life is not a coincidence; life is a consequence.

Tony, a young man I met on a trip to the Midwest, told me about an idea he had for a business that would match individuals or families with the best pets for them. He worked at an animal shelter, and every day people would return pets or drop off ones they had purchased from a breeder or a pet store because the animal and the person or family did not mesh well. From his work with animals (and people) he knew a way to find just the right type of pet for individual types of people. What a phenomenal idea! This business would reduce pet dumping, abuse, regret, and returns, and increase the happiness of both people and animals.

He told me all about this great idea, but when I asked him what he had done to make it a reality, he told me he hadn't done any work yet. "I'm going to start in the next few months," he said. Okay. When I was back in the Midwest a few months later, I ran into Tony and asked him about the progress he had made on the pet-matching business. His answer: none. "I'm starting next month," he said.

I asked Tony how he spent his days. He began them like many of us do—by checking e-mail and then logging on to Facebook, Twitter, Reddit, and Instagram for "five minutes." Before he knew it, two hours had passed and it was time for him to get to the shelter to work. When he got home at night, he'd have dinner with his family, watch the news, and check in on his favorite teams either on TV or online. By that time, he was too tired to do anything else, so he'd "veg out" and promise himself that tomorrow he'd make headway on his business idea. The cycle repeated itself the next day, and the day after that. "Later" was quickly becoming "never."

That's not going to work. To get anything done effectively—and to combat procrastination—you need to put some firm practices into place. Here are a few ways I encourage people to stop making excuses and take control of their time:

* *Spend the first thirty minutes of your day working, not checking.* If you need to check e-mail or your social news sites, do it only after you have established a good work groove. In Tony's case, he needed to get up in the morning and spend thirty minutes working on his business plan. To do so, he made sure the Internet and e-mail programs were turned off on his computer.

* *Make a list and do the first thing on it.* Starting anything new can be hard, but if you can get over that hump, you will gain momentum and be more likely to keep at it. "One thing leads to another" is an old saw for a reason—it's true. Lists are great for getting things done now, and you can thank something called the Zeigarnik effect, which states that unfinished tasks are more likely to get stuck in your memory. A to-do list calms the Zeigarnik effect and helps you check off the boxes more easily.

* *Break down big jobs into small ones.* Big tasks (starting a pet-matching business) can be daunting and therefore easy to put aside for another time. Break the big job into smaller, finite ones. Tony's small tasks included coming up with a name for the business, a mission statement, and a list of required resources and materials. After that, he was on his way.

* *Be nice.* If you've already procrastinated, research shows you're more likely to get started on time this time if you show yourself compassion for past slacking phases and don't beat

yourself up about them—that just increases the risk of procrastination.

* *Remind yourself why you want to do it.* If you struggle to get something done, spend some time reminding yourself why you want to do it and why it is so important. This was easy for Tony: every day he saw people abandoning or returning pets they could not care for because they were bad matches. Assigning personal meaning to a task makes you more likely to tackle it and avoid procrastination.

* *If the timing isn't right, figure out why and do it anyway.* If you are putting off doing something and telling yourself that the time isn't right, ask yourself why. There could be a legitimate reason to put something off, but most of the time there isn't. You can always do something to move forward with a plan. Twitter creator Jack Dorsey had the idea for the social networking site in 2000. At the time, the technology that would help Twitter succeed was not a reality; Dorsey knew this because he did a very small-scale and low-risk version of Twitter that failed. However, the attempt also showed him that when the technology did exist, his idea would have merit. When that time came, he already had the groundwork in place and was able to hit the ground running.

Evaluate Yourself on Output, Not on Activity

I have a colleague who would become very excited when starting a project—his enthusiasm was palpable. At the beginning, he would gather his materials, make lists, reach out to partners, make phone calls—a flurry of activity that made a whirling dervish look slow. Inevitably, as time went on, my friend's enthusiasm for the project would begin to wane. Tasks would remain unfinished, phones calls would go unreturned for days and sometimes weeks. The project would sometimes be passed off to an underling to finish and some projects would just remain undone in favor of the excitement of something new. There was no interest in completion—in the process that takes a brilliant idea to final product. My friend remained constantly busy, but his productivity was dismal. He would be the first to tell you how hardworking he was, but he had very little to show for it. He measured himself on activity, not on output. Baseball players get paid to hit the ball, not just swing at it.

The same can be said of people who spend half the day answering e-mails and reading and engaging in social media. These are activities that can't be monetized, they don't result in anything concrete. Yet people spend so much of their day on these time sucks that they wonder why they are "busy" and never accomplish half of what they set out to do in a twelve-hour period.

When I wake up in the morning I think about what I can do for the next few hours that will forward my career, get me closer to a professional or personal goal, or help me finish a project. E-mail, social media, and nonurgent phone calls can all wait until after I have accomplished the tasks that are the most profitable, such as going over shooting schedules and programming notes, looking at any pending contracts or potential business agreements, checking ratings and audience engagement statistics, and returning priority phone calls.

You can move a hundred pieces of paper every day, but if it doesn't make any money or get you closer to a goal, it is pointless busywork. Being active without accomplishing anything has real consequences, as I explained earlier. It's easy to get stuck in this pattern—days and then weeks and months and even years pass, and before you know it, the strategic plan you've been thinking about has not been implemented, the novel you wanted to write remains just a thought, and the triathlon you wanted to run this year has come and gone. You never got to where you thought you were going. How many goals have you wanted to reach that still remain pipe dreams?

I am sure you have a to-do list. My guess is that it has a mix of items that range from the practical (pick up dry cleaning, buy dog food) to the timely (get the quarterly report done, pay taxes) to the lofty (write the screenplay, learn Italian). How many of these items do you check off at the end of the day? The dry cleaning and the dog food? Okay, great. Did they get you any closer to your real goals? You have to check in with yourself at the end of each day to see if you actually accomplished anything important. Did you have meaningful output, or were you busy all day running errands, pushing paper, and bitching about your workload to colleagues?

We tend to get stuck on procedures and busywork—when we need to stop doing those things and work hard on our lives. If all day you are doing busywork, when do you find the time to better your situation? At what point do you start working *on* your life? You have to allocate time to make your life better, whether it's half an hour learning something new, as we talked about in the last chapter, or spending half an hour a day on the novel you want to write so that it will get done. If we allow errands to take over our future, we will have no future. All we have is today. We need to identify that just being in our lives is not enough; it's when we work on our lives that life improves.

I know of a woman, Alanna, who owns a framing shop in a very prosperous, populated town. Opening her own gallery and framing shop was a lifelong dream, and she did it. The business is running well too, but now she's drowning in back orders. She tells me she is busy all day and cannot get to all her orders on time. Customers are starting to become frustrated.

When I quizzed Alanna more deeply and asked her what exactly she did the day before we spoke, she told me she made ten phone calls, ordered seventeen frames, read forty-seven e-mails and responded to about half of them (deleting the other, nonessential half), met with three customers and took their orders, ate lunch, ran an errand, looked at her social media pages, checked the news online, and framed one photograph.

All of this was done between the time the shop opened at ten a.m. and when it closed at five p.m. Alanna told me she was exhausted at the end of the day. I am sure she *was* tired, not least because she knew she did not do the framing that she wanted, and needed, to do. Not getting real stuff done hangs over your head like the sword of Damocles—and it is stressful, depressing, and tiring.

Alanna is in the business of framing, yet she managed to frame only one image *during one day of work*. She measured her day in terms of activity. I told her she needed to start measuring her output, not her activity. She needed to think about how many framings she could complete in one day, working the same hours she was already working. I told her to try an experiment: for one day she should put everything, except lunch, on the back burner. Her task would be to go into work and frame as many pictures as she could using the state-of-the-art automated machinery she owns that makes cutting mats and assembling frames fairly quick work. The next day she tried my strategy and managed to frame up ten pictures. The day after that, she framed twelve. She did this for a week, and by Saturday she was nearly caught up on her back orders.

Did any of the other activities suffer because she started measuring herself on output of her business's central function? No. The fact is, the activities that took all day (e-mail, social media, phone calls, monitoring the news) could be accomplished in a matter of about sixty to ninety minutes. When she changed her thinking from activity to output, the way Alanna spent her day shifted. I know many successful people who check e-mail only once in the morning and once in the afternoon. They scan the news when they wake up and before they go to bed at night. They make phone calls for a certain limited amount of time in the morning, and follow up in the afternoon during a prescribed period if necessary. In other words, they enhance their output with a routine, and by valuing output over activity. They know what they need to get done to move their day and their career forward—all the rest is gravy.

Balls in the Air:
Manage Priorities, Not Errands

Like Alanna, most of us *don't* have to work fifteen, nineteen, or twenty hours a day to meet our goals. We probably don't even have to work twelve hours a day. There are people who run billion-dollar businesses in twelve hours a day or less, go home to their families, and manage to get a good night's sleep. The major difference between an efficient person's day and your day is the ability to prioritize.

I wake up ninety minutes before I have to leave my house so I can eat breakfast, check the news and e-mail, and have some breathing room before I start the day. I am dressed in five minutes because I know what I am going to wear; my wardrobe is simple and prepared. I define each day by what I need to accomplish—I am priority driven. I know what will take me forward and what will keep me stalled.

Even if you have twenty different things going on, you may not necessarily have to cut back on them to be efficient. You just have to figure out what your priorities are on a daily basis because it's unlikely that you can work on all twenty tasks in one day—or work on them very effectively.

Brian Wansink directs the Cornell Food and Brand Lab. He coined the term "mindless eating" (and wrote a bestseller by the same name).[4] He describes mindless eating as a kind of overeating caused by distractions, among which he includes certain types of packaging, the colors and lighting around us, even family and friends. I think we can describe mindless activity in the same way—it's stuff you do when you're not really paying attention and under the influence of outside factors that distract you or people who don't always have your best interests in mind.

Instead of allowing yourself to binge on junk activity (as opposed to junk food, which you should not binge on either), shift your thinking from time management to *priority management.* I think of all the things I have to get done as balls. I might have twenty balls, but only five are really important on any given day. I have to move those fives balls every day. After a certain number of days, I will push those balls over the finish line and another five will take their place. If I can move each of those balls each day, I am progressing my life and my agenda. If those balls don't move, I'm not moving. I wake up energized by the ball that will be hardest to move and excited about the one easiest to move. Winners go for the tough balls first.

One of my major balls is getting *Bar Rescue* done in a tight time frame. We used to shoot an entire episode in five days, with thirty-six hours for remodeling within those five days. Now we shoot the entire episode in four days (still with thirty-six hours for remodeling). We arrive at a location in the afternoon for a two-hour session that is filmed, and then we have two full days to fully rebrand and renovate the bar. On the fourth day, shooting is completed by the afternoon, which ends with the reveal and a reopening of the "new" bar. Essentially, I have only two full days and two half days to turn a place around. That includes retraining staff, cleaning, fixing anything that is broken, renovating the concept and any branding, and recipe development. There are many parts to the effort. In the time crunch we face, understanding which balls are important and which ones are less so is crucial. Choose the wrong balls and you're screwed. You have to compartmentalize and see how each ball functions in the overall goal for the day, week, and month.

What can you do today that will bring you closer to where you want to be tomorrow? Those are the balls you move. Focus on two or three of the most important tasks with an eye toward completion. Ask yourself the following:

* *What can I make progress on today (aspects of major projects)?* For example, if you are working toward becoming a real estate agent, you have to take a certain number of courses in order to get your license. It's different for each state, so if you haven't done so, find out what your state requires, and then sign up for the courses. If you're taking those courses already, you might have to work on finding a broker to work with because that is also a requirement in order to practice as an agent. You need to contact a broker *before* graduating from training.

* *What can I actually finish today (important tasks that won't take more than a couple of hours)?* Keeping with the real estate theme, you can study for your courses or for the exam, do your real estate course homework, or research and send letters to the brokers you've identified.
* *What can I get out of the way in a short, prescribed period of time (must-do tasks, like returning or making phone calls or answering e-mails)?* This is the time you take for "administrative" tasks, like returning a broker's call, or any other short task. Time and priority management are as much about what you *are not* going to do today than what you *are* going to do.

Examine how you organize your day. That means making a note of what you do each hour using a chart or preprinted day-planner pages broken up into hours. It's the same technique financial experts recommend for getting your personal finances in order—write down what you buy and how much you spend. At the end of the week or month, it is very eye-opening to see how much money you actually did not have to spend. You gain a clear picture of why you have no money left at the end of a month. Same thing goes for time. Do this for a week and you will see a pattern emerge—what you think you're spending your time on versus what you actually do all day.

Once you have this information from your time deep dive, you can turn it into personally actionable steps. Rather than hap-hazardly adding to your workload or randomly putting off some projects in favor of others, analyze how much leadership, attention, guidance, and intervention each project needs. How much oversight is truly required? What projects and tasks can you delegate?

You can make this a regular habit in about twenty-one days, a theory I discuss on page 93, the amount of time it takes to make most changes permanent. We'll meet people who have successfully reduced time wasting and now live balanced, full lives—and accomplish more too.

In terms of my own career, when I shifted my priorities from working as a hospitality consultant (a role I did and do excel at) to developing a television show, the way I used my time changed. I was now no longer just thinking about creating a television show; I *was* creating a television show. My priority became working on the show, not working on my consulting and thinking about a show. That is a significant difference, which led to a significant change in my behavior. Suddenly, instead of just talking about a TV show, I started doing what was necessary to make a show happen. I had a purpose. I shot sizzle reels—visual representations of my personality and the key concepts of the show—wrote a description of what the show would be about and who would be in it, worked on meeting and creating relationships with producers, and zeroed in on other activities that would bring me closer to my goal. I increased my output of tasks that brought me closer to getting a show on air. Despite all the odds, it worked. I did develop a show and it was picked up. *Bar Rescue* continues to grow and evolve.

Delegate

There may also be things on your to-do list that other people can handle more quickly and efficiently than you can. You may be wasting an enormous amount of time on such tasks. The first things to delegate are those that you dislike doing, that you dread and put off, or that you aren't very good at. This could be anything from ironing shirts to transcribing tapes to researching background for a business you're working on. I call these low-payoff activities that must be done but can be done better by someone else at a lower personal and professional cost to you. That way you can focus on high-payoff tasks that you *do* enjoy and that have a larger benefit for you. Virgin Group founder Richard Branson, who describes himself as both dyslexic and having ADHD, attributes his ability to produce and innovate to delegation. "As much as you need a strong personality to build a business from scratch, you also must understand the art of delegation," says Branson. "I have to be good at helping people run the individual businesses, and I have to be willing to step back. The company must be set up so it can continue without me."[5]

Apply Branson's wisdom to your own life, whether you own a business or work an office job, by allowing others to take over tasks that take you away from meeting major goals. Many businesspeople use what is called the 70 percent rule. I'm not sure who coined the term, but it's a way of figuring out what you can and can't delegate. If someone can do a task at least 70 percent as well as you can (and maybe even better), delegate the task to that person. In real life, some things need to be done to 100 percent perfection, but many tasks don't have to be, and 70 percent may be just right.

If you can hire even part-time help with delegation, take advantage of it. That said, you have to trust the people you hire to follow through on tasks because the whole point of paying someone to do something for you is to give you more time to work on priorities, not less time because you are cleaning up their messes. I can't give you a seminar on hiring here, but briefly, rather than relying on job descriptions that simply quantify duties and correlating them with matching experience, I use a more holistic approach. I think of eight adjectives and descriptive phrases for the person I want in a particular role, one to whom I can delegate tasks that have passed the 70 percent rule. What kind of person can do those kinds of things? This gets you thinking about an actual type of person rather than a faceless list of qualifications.

Next, properly describe the role. When asking people about referrals or even advertising for someone in a classified ad, describe the ideal person with those adjectives. Keep the application as simple as possible, limiting requirements to the absolute minimum you would need before getting a feel for the candidate in an in-person interview.

If a person's personality and interpersonal skills seem right—and I consider only candidates who fulfill at least six out of the eight adjectives—then (and only then) her past experience becomes relevant to the discussion. That's because I believe you can train people to do a job but you cannot teach them to have the right personality for it. Keep your list of adjectives in front of you when meeting with the person, and make note of those that fit. I use the "three Cs" as the foundation of an interview: I have a *conversation* with her by asking questions that require expressive answers; I demonstrate *conviction* about my company and the job I am offering to gauge if her passion matches mine; and I show *curiosity* about her.

Once you have someone whom you can delegate tasks to, make sure you are very clear about what you want done so the person can start the task and not need to ask a lot of follow-up questions. Set a deadline and some kind of feedback system, which can be as simple as asking the person to text or e-mail you when the job is done. When I use my system of balls, I always attach one of my balls to a person who can help me move it. That way we own the ball together and it gets moved more easily. For example, my producers help me move the *Bar Rescue* balls, my writer Karen helps me move my book balls, my assistant helps me move my office balls, and so on.

If you cannot afford to hire a staff or an assistant, consider hiring someone part time. A good part-time person can often be found using Craigslist or other resources at surprisingly affordable fees. This is especially true if you live in a small town, where stay-at-home moms and retired people (with a lot of skills) may be very happy for the extra money and work—and they are often very competent. Or leverage technology. Consider virtual assistants, people who live far from you but can handle a variety of tasks remotely, as another affordable option. There are also teleconferencing services, time-tracking tools, online invoicing services, remote desktop applications, online scheduling help, and many other Internet-based services that can help you become more efficient and eliminate mundane tasks.

Delegating may take some work, but it's very often worth it.

Stop Thinking of Family as a Time Suck

I often hear time-related excuses around family. For example: "I don't have time to work because I have two kids," or "My family is preventing me from succeeding."

Not only do these excuses keep you from accomplishing things you actually do have time for, they can also be very hard on family relationships, because people who use these kinds of excuses often allow resentment toward their family to grow.

No matter what kind of job you have, your family comes first. Yes, it is extra work, but it's part of the package. I raised a daughter while doing a great deal of long-distance travel, including grueling trips to Asia. My daughter and I had an arrangement—she faxed me her homework at five a.m. my time, which was five p.m. where she was. I would call her and go over it with her every day. I chose to do this because it was the right thing to do to build our relationship and be a good father. And we managed to make this work across the globe before the Internet and Skype made real-time communication accessible from anywhere. I know firsthand that the idea that you can't take care of both business and family is a lie.

One bar owner I worked with, Will, thought he had no time to spend with his family, and his business suffered because he was too tired to really focus on what needed to be done. Will would get home at four a.m., sleep until noon, wake up, shower, dress, and go straight to his bar. I know corporate guys who work like this too. They stay late at work, get home after their kids are in bed, go to work again before the kids get up, and repeat. Are they thriving at work? Hell, no. Is their family thriving without them? Uh-uh. It's no way to live.

When Will came to me for advice, we sat down and looked at what he was doing at the bar. Many tasks were a waste of his time, and we decided that other people could easily handle them. Now he leaves the bar for two hours in the early evening to have dinner with his family. He entrusts someone else to do the closing of the bar, so he gets home closer to midnight, which means he can get up earlier and spend time with his family in the morning.

Rather than saying "I am too busy," say, "I don't have the capacity to handle every single aspect of owning and running this business." That's okay. Sure, you should know how to perform every task related to your business, or at least understand the responsibilities. However, that does not mean you should try to do everything or micromanage others. How can you grow and expand, innovate and evolve, if you are *doing* rather than *managing*? You can't. Once you admit this to yourself and change the way you talk about what you need to do, you can look for ways to change your day and your work style.

Bullshit Buster: Peter Shankman

Peter Shankman—serial entrepreneur, founder of the journalist Web site HARO (Help a Reporter Out), and author of several books, including *Faster Than Normal*—knows it can be tough to make time to focus on the hard stuff. In fact, it's probably more difficult for Peter, because he has ADHD. Still, he doesn't allow time to get the better of him and has worked out ways of using his ADHD to his advantage. In 2015, he recalls, he was facing down a deadline for turning in his next book. "My publisher was getting antsy, as I hadn't sent her anything yet. I'd done all the research; the problem was sitting down and banging it out," Peter says. "Yet I wasn't worried. I'd been there before. With twelve days left until my deadline, I went to the United Airlines Web site and bought a round-trip business-class ticket to Tokyo leaving the next day. I got on the plane armed with nothing but my laptop, a power cord, and my phone."

When the plane took off, Peter took out his laptop, and in the fourteen hours it took to get from Newark to Tokyo, he wrote chapters 1 through 5. "After landing in Tokyo, I went through immigration, walked outside, took a deep breath of fresh air, turned around, went back through security to the gate, and boarded the same plane back to Newark. I even sat in the same seat," he says. On the twelve-hour flight home, Peter wrote chapters 6 through 10. He landed back home thirty-one hours after taking off with a completed book—and his second bestseller—in hand.

When Peter tells this story to most people, they look at him like he might be nuts. After all, what kind of person would spend upward of five thousand dollars on a round-trip flight just to have a space to write in order to meet a deadline in twelve days? As Peter explains, he found a system that works for him. "Being on a plane in a comfortable seat makes me a captive audience of my own obligations and goals."

Peter knows he is never going to take nine months to write a book, methodically spending a few hours each day getting a few thousand words down on paper. That's not the way he rolls; that style of time management doesn't work for him. It's not that he hadn't been working on it—the book had been percolating and forming in his mind for a long time. When he finally got in the plane seat, it all came forward and he was able to write the book in what most people consider to be an intense time frame. The quality of the book didn't suffer, as it might for someone else using the same technique. Because Peter's brain works in a way that is different from that of someone who does not have ADHD, he produced something good.

Peter's story points to the importance of knowing yourself and using strategies that suit your style and personality instead of using it as an excuse to not get your work done. "Thinking differently helps, as does realizing that what other people think of me doesn't matter, as long as I'm happy with myself," Peter says. "I focus my time on doing things that improve my life. I'm a constant reinvention of myself, always striving for the next great thing. In the end, the goal is to create, build, and keep myself occupied with things that work for me, so I'm focused on doing positive things, as opposed to focusing on those things that could negatively affect me."

That means using whatever tools he can, both digital and analog, to run his life and make it as productive as possible. "I'm always discovering new strategies to up my productivity that don't include flying to Tokyo and back. Still, I see five thousand dollars as a small and very good investment in my productivity and success. A lot of people spend more money than that trying to get things done and don't come close to writing a book in less than thirty-six hours."

Bullshit Buster: Jeff Ganz

Jeff Ganz (www.jeffganz.com) and I go back a long time. Jeff was fifteen years old and I was fourteen years old when we were in a band together. We would rehearse in my basement. Jeff could play the guitar like Jimi Hendrix—with his teeth, behind his back, even upside down. Even then I knew he was an incredible musician. I was right—he went on to tour and record with such legends as Johnny Winter, Lou Reed, Tito Puente, Chuck Berry, the Village People, Rita Moreno, Gerry Mulligan, and many others.

It's hard to imagine that procrastination could be even a remote possibility for someone as accomplished and enthusiastic as Jeff. However, he tells me it was actually the way he wound up figuring out what he really wanted to do with his musical career.

Jeff taught himself to play guitar as a kid in the dormitory at a private boarding school. By the time he was nineteen he was known as a very good rock guitar player and vocalist in the style of Jimi Hendrix and Eric Clapton. He later learned the Great American Songbook. When we were a bit older, we ended up doing gigs with a local band on Long Island.

Jeff was an accomplished guitar player, but he didn't have the same passion for it that he had had as a kid—and he wasn't spending as much time practicing. When he was twenty, he met a guitarist and arranger (who later became a famous film composer), who gave him his first lesson on the bass. At that point everything changed for him. As Jeff says, "I did not want to know everything about the guitar, but I did want to know everything about the bass. It was a moment of clarity for me. It was clear to me that I was procrastinating with the guitar because I truly wasn't interested in it. Had I not become a bass player, switched over from guitar, and realized the history of music is as important as the music of the present and future, I am not sure I would be as successful as I am today. After I made the switch to the bass, I did not procrastinate. I found the back meaning of songs. I was deeply interested in the music I was playing on the bass. Everything is different if you know the reasons for things. For me, knowing more equals procrastinating less. I am truly interested in what I'm learning. I want to be true to my craft. That's what motivates me and keeps me from procrastinating."

Jeff went on to master not only the traditional upright bass but also the fretted and fretless four-, five-, and eight-string electric bass as well as the fretted and fretless acoustic bass guitar and piccolo bass. He's become a go-to guy in many genres and has toured the world with amazing performers. Not bad for someone who once felt he was wasting time in music.

Now he has different reasons to avoid procrastination. "Being a husband, stepfather, and grandfather means I procrastinate less because those responsibilities make my mortality more apparent. I am not playing for the same reason I was when I was eighteen. I don't feel I am competing with anyone; every gig I have gotten I have not chased. When you are doing what you love and being who you love, a lot of serendipity comes into play."

It's time to break the time-excuse habit. It can be done.

There is a theory that changing human behavior takes twenty-one cycles (actually, it was a plastic surgeon, Maxwell Maltz, who originally noticed the twenty-one-day phenomenon back in the 1950s).[6] Quitting smoking takes twenty-one days of abstinence; changing a pattern at work takes twenty-one shifts; learning to make exercise a regular habit takes twenty-one visits to the gym. It may take you twenty-one days to end your habit of bad time management and faulty prioritizing because those mistakes have become chronic. Use whatever tools you can to focus on what is important. Whether it's taking a long plane ride that forces you to get something done or being honest with yourself about what you like to do and don't like to do, it's now or never. You never get back the time you wasted.

If you've been putting off a task or action, do it now. There's no better time.

DBY To-Do List

* Value your time properly. You have twenty-four hours each day, and then *poof!* The day is over. It's time to start respecting the limited time you have by giving it the importance it deserves. Use your time wisely on things that matter and that

bring you joy and happiness, propel you forward, and help you reach your goals.

* Delegate. There are things you are not good at, don't like doing, are a waste of your time, and could be done better, faster, and more cheaply by others. What are they? Figure it out and stop wasting your own time on these tasks.

* Stop procrastinating. Here's a quick version of my five-step plan: Spend the first thirty minutes of your day working, not checking social media and e-mail. Make a list and do the top priority on it. Break down big jobs into small ones, then do each job one step at a time. Remind yourself why you want to do it. If the timing isn't right, figure out why and do it anyway.

* Evaluate yourself on output, not activity. When assessing how you spent your day, look at what you actually accomplished, not the amount of busywork you did. This helps with rule number one, valuing your time.

* **Manage priorities**. Look at what needs to be done to meet your goals strategically. Make sure you are doing tasks in the right order, which is the order that brings you to your goal the most efficiently.

* Stop thinking of family as a time suck. Your family doesn't take up your time! Time spent with family is never a waste—make it meaningful and high quality. It pays dividends in the amounts of joy and enthusiasm you have in life.

Chapter 4

✱

EXCUSE #4:
CIRCUMSTANCES

"People are always blaming their circumstances for what they are. I don't believe in circumstances. The people who get on in this world are the people who get up and look for the circumstances they want, and, if they can't find them, make them."

—George Bernard Shaw, Irish playwright and critic

Excuses Based Around External Factors That Cannot Be Changed or Are Difficult to Change

Let's get something straight at the outset of this chapter: unavoidable or unchangeable circumstances do not prevent you from accomplishing goals or succeeding.

Some excuse makers think blaming circumstances—any external factors that you didn't choose but that you need to deal with—gives them a pass on facing their reality. If you can't find a good janitor, the thinking goes, then you don't have to worry about how clean your establishment is—you have no control over it anyway. You don't have to take the necessary actions to improve what's wrong, because the factors outside your control, such as the weather or the greater economic situation or the hiring pool, get in your way. Exigent circumstances may be challenging to deal with, but they aren't impossible to address.

When you think that an external circumstance cannot be gotten around, you are engaging in magical thinking. I believe in God, but I don't think He's ruining my business on purpose, or making it snow or rain to teach me a lesson. Magical thinking, in general, is an absolutely absurd way to think of your failings because it's truly all in your head. It's a huge obstacle in terms of identifying fixable problems in your business and life. I cannot believe that anyone could seriously suggest that God wants us to do anything else but succeed. Just because it was a very cold winter and you lost money doesn't mean the universe conspired against you. Guess what? Snow in the winter is pretty predictable in parts of the country where it, er, *snows in the winter.* You can and should prepare for the inevitable and stop blaming luck or magic for your failures and indecision.

To prove that the excuses of weather and other natural phenomena are all in your head, I'll tell you about one establishment I ran in Seattle, Washington. I would get daily sales reports, and on the top line of each report, the managers would record that day's "Weather / Business Conditions." In January, poor business was blamed on cold weather. If it rained, managers blamed the bad performance on rain. (Frankly, hospitality businesses, especially bars, should do pretty damn good business when it's pouring outside—where else are you going to go?) One day I saw that the low sales were blamed on "the first sunny day." I asked the manager, "Let me get this straight: the weather is an excuse when it is raining or cold, but it's also an excuse when it's beautiful outside?"

When you hear yourself saying . . .

* ★ My physical condition prevents me from fulfilling my dreams.
* ★ The neighborhood is bad.
* ★ The demographics are wrong for my business.
* ★ My location is bad.
* ★ There are no good people around to hire.
* ★ The weather destroys my chances for success.
* ★ Government policies make it impossible for me to be profitable.
* ★ My competition is killing me.

. . . it's time to face your circumstance excuses and stop bullshitting yourself!

Immediately after that, I removed the "Weather / Business Conditions" line from my sales reports and forbade the staff from talking about the weather. Weather is inconsequential to success. That line, in fact, made it easier for them to make excuses! Your job is to entice customers to your business and fill the place every day. I don't care if you work in a car dealership, a restaurant, a dress store, in the professional services industry, or at a corporate job. You have to stop blaming out-of-your-control circumstances for your misfortune. You can't control the weather, your competition, or the neighborhood demographics, but you *can* control your responses to these things.

If you are in a region where it snows every winter, how about having a winter warm-up party or a heavy-socks party? These sorts of gimmicks work well in retail and hospitality. I took the weather and made it part of our shtick instead of using it as an excuse. I opened an outdoor deck bar at the bar in Seattle. Everyone told me I was nuts because it rains so much there. We ended up having the most successful happy hour in town because we set up these really amazing, huge umbrellas that protected people from the rain while still allowing them to have a great time. We called it Umbrella Hour (of course!). It was a matter of taking a circumstance excuse—"the rain ruins my business"—and turning it into what it is: a predictable condition that can become a true advantage. Remember, almost everything can become an asset.

I rescued a once-popular dance club, Rocks, which had fallen on hard times after a California smoking law changed and patrons were no longer allowed to light up inside the bar. Rocks owner Scott Terheggen said this new law made it impossible for his bar to be successful because smoking was its key feature. How crazy is that? Yet that was Scott's excuse! Laws and regulations change *all* the time and you must adapt. Scott used the smoking law as a crutch. Smoking wasn't the only reason people liked Scott's dance club—and not having smoking in the bar would be an attraction to a whole group of people who loved to dance but couldn't stand the stench of cigarettes.

Most of the existing patrons came to have a great time on the dance floor anyway. Scott had to stop blaming the club's failings on the circumstance of California smoking laws. In fact, I say Scott should have seen that the days of smoking in bars in

California were numbered. We reinvigorated the bar's dance club vibe by updating its look and playing up an industrial-loft feel that was contemporary and unique. We also made sure the bar was cleaned thoroughly so that no stale odors remained. "No smoking" went from being a lousy excuse to an incredible asset. From 2009 to 2014 the bar thrived, and now Scott focuses on its two other branches in California, one in Norwalk and the other in Long Beach, which continue to thrive—without smoking!

Take a Second Look

"It's the economy, stupid" is another form of "That's the way things are" thinking I hear quite often. It sounds insurmountable, doesn't it? That's an excuse you can coast on for quite a while. Still, anyone can figure out a way to work with the economic situation he is faced with. It's called turning an obstacle into an asset.

David C. McCourt, the founder and CEO of Granahan McCourt Capital, is a telecommunications and cable entrepreneur and investor. McCourt says it's a losing battle to try to change reality; he cites the music industry as one example. He says the industry's threats to sue Internet companies were based on magical thinking because they ultimately failed. Instead, he says, music companies needed to build an economic world around how people were consuming music. Instead of trying to stop the flow of content—which was never going to happen—the music and other media companies that asked "How can I help sort through the noise of all that content?" survived.

The question you should always ask yourself is, How can I take the existing environment or condition and adapt to it so I can serve existing stakeholders and attract new ones? If you don't have customers in the conventional sense, ask, How can I respond to current conditions to elevate my ability to do my job? Even better is asking, What are the ways I can get ahead of the curve and anticipate what people will want next? You should be thinking about the future, not how to maintain the status quo. Media companies that shifted into the new reality of music consumption won, and those that didn't or wouldn't lost.

What does this mean for you? You have to see unchangeable circumstances not as obstacles that allow you to give up but as challenges and opportunities to try new ways of doing things.

You have to stop thinking you are where you used to be and deal with the here and now. That often requires you to take a second, and sometimes a third, look at your surroundings and any changes that are taking place. Kathy owned a dress shop in a small upstate New York town that has both a year-round and a seasonal population. She'd been there for twenty years and business had declined despite having a fantastic location: it's in a small, historic complex that was formerly a gristmill. It also holds a popular restaurant/bar and a country store that sells local products and home-decorating items. Directly across the street sits a large multidealer antiques store, a pet-supply shop, a yoga studio, and a busy pizza parlor. Kathy firmly placed the blame for falling sales on a difficult customer base. Ultimately, she decided to sell the lease and was shocked when, six months later, she visited the store and learned that Lori, the new owner, had doubled her sales every month and was planning on breaking down a wall in the back of the store so that she could expand!

"I don't get it," Kathy said to Lori. "Where do you find the customers?"

"They are right here, right in town," said Lori. "I just figured out who they were and what they wanted, and I try my best to provide that. They love leggings, fun and inexpensive jewelry, scarves, kimonos, dresses and tops that can be layered, and items made from easy-care, washable fabrics."

In other words, it wasn't the customers, it was the clothes! Kathy had not changed her clothing strategy since she opened in the late 1990s. The more formal, higher-priced items she had been selling weren't desirable to the majority of women in town. She never bothered to find out how the demographics had changed and how she might adapt in terms of her inventory. The first thing Lori did, before she even decided to take the lease on the building, was talk to local real estate agents about who were buying houses (young families) and who were selling them (retirees fleeing the cold for warmer locales). She studied clothing trends and walked around the local malls and her favorite boutiques to see what was selling. Once established, Kathy didn't think she had to do that— she thought she understood her customers even though they had aged out and left the area.

Even office workers can overcome institutional obstacles. Dan works in IT for a large bakery that bakes large numbers of cookies, breads, and crackers. He had a great idea for a virtual reality tour of the factory that would show consumers how cookies and other items were made as if they themselves were in the mixing bowl and on the conveyer belt. He knew that virtual reality tours had become a big business, and he saw it as a great way to capture consumer delight and loyalty, upping brand recognition and ultimately increasing consumption.

Dan developed a prototype for the VR tour and was absolutely certain that his boss would approve the idea. Well, his boss *didn't* like the idea and his "No" was still ringing in Dan's ears when he sat back down in his cubicle. The *no* was a pretty big obstacle, but Dan was not deterred. He thought that maybe his boss just didn't like his particular approach to the idea. He looked at it again and tackled it in a different way. He knew at least one thing his boss didn't like about it, so he changed the way the VR tour directed the viewer through the cookie-making process, hoping that if the boss didn't like plan A, maybe he'd like plan B.

However, Dan's boss did not like plan B either. Dan was starting to think that maybe his boss just didn't like him, especially because a VR tour of a cookie factory, with the viewer as the cookie, seemed pretty damn cool to Dan and to friends with whom he had shared the prototype. Now what? Two *no*'s in a row seemed like a pretty big obstacle. Time to give up? Third time might not be the charm, but it might result in a pink slip.

Dan decided to accept the *no* he could not change and looked at it as an opportunity. He realized that the double *no* actually gave Dan permission to pursue the idea in other ways. He took it and turned it into two choices: develop the VR tour on his own or use it as entrée to a new job at a different company. Dan took the second option. With good conscience he pitched the idea to a rival cookie company, and they loved the idea, which is now in development. In addition, Dan no longer sits in a cubicle. His office space has four walls, a window, and a door. I don't know if this tour will ever be offered to the public, but it doesn't matter—Dan took an obstacle and turned it into a new and better job where people listen to his ideas and take them seriously.

Remember that successful, excuse-free people work *with* what they have at hand; they research conditions and adapt to them; they take information, even if it is negative, and figure out how they can use that knowledge to better themselves.

Blaming failures on outside circumstances or other people can negatively affect self-discipline and lead to more negative actions. This makes sense, because if you feel you aren't in control of what happens in your business, and you see bad things that happen as the fault of things and people you can't control, where is the incentive to improve and apply yourself? There isn't any.

Harvard Business School researchers Christopher G. Myers, Bradley R. Staats, and Francesca Gino found that when there is an opportunity to blame our failures on external factors instead of our own actions, we jump at the chance to do so.[1] Further, when we are unaccountable, we don't learn. Do you see how so many of the major excuse categories are interconnected? It's scary! Don't be a victim of your bullshit.

This study reminds me of a guy I knew when I was bartending at Barney's Beanery in Los Angeles in the late 1970s. Hank was such a loser—he would sit at the bar and complain that the mistakes he made at work were management's fault. He couldn't make his quota (he worked in a factory) because the floor manager busted his balls too often for him to focus. Hank was docked coming back late from lunch because "the commissary was not run properly and it took too long to get a sandwich." This blame game was old in 1979 and it should be ancient history today. If you blame external conditions rather than your own missteps and bad decisions, you're less likely to learn from your mistakes and make better decisions next time. That was certainly the case for Hank. He never changed his behavior, and last I heard, he was out of a job. What a terrible, wasteful way to spend your life.

It's hard not to take ownership of failure. It's human nature, after all, and sometimes you might be working with a team of different personalities and unpredictable factors, like iffy technology, or even natural events, like a major storm, that can affect outcomes. So how do you prevent yourself from inaction in these circumstances?

Christopher Myers, one of the Harvard study researchers, told the *Harvard Business Review* that it's important to foster a culture where it is okay to acknowledge and learn from circumstances and failure, but without encouraging external blame.[2] In other words, you can say, "The weather is lousy and I am going to devise a plan so next time it rains, it doesn't prevent me from succeeding," and so on. It's also important to create an environment where failures and obstacles are seen as opportunities to grow, not occasions for dodging responsibility.

Here's how:

* Always give a situation a second or third look. Reexamining existing conditions allows you more time to see things differently.
* Ask yourself what a particular obstacle is telling you. What information can you glean from the situation so that you can turn it to your advantage, like Lori did in terms of understanding her customers and Dan did when he took his VR cookie tour to another company?
* Understand why something failed. Can you remove those components and go back to the drawing board with what's left?

Come On, Get Happy

If you have a tendency to see all or most barriers as impenetrable to your success and well-being, you have to do a little work to change that tendency. Happiness and positive psychology expert

Martin Seligman at the University of Pennsylvania says that optimists treat failure as learning experiences and believe they can do better next time. If you're not naturally optimistic, that's okay—you can actually practice being optimistic, says Seligman. Once you do, you will be less likely to see obstacles as permanent and the cause of your problems.

There are six different ways you can practice being optimistic and less swayed by what you cannot control:

1. *Stop putting so much stock into what other people think.* Of course we should listen and consider others' opinions, but we also have to understand where those opinions are coming from and whether what people say really holds true. If Kara Goldin had listened to a major soda company executive when he told her an unsweetened beverage would never work because Americans will consume only sweet drinks, she would never have started her profitable beverage company, Hint Water.

2. *Don't use toxic people and situations as an excuse for toxic reactions.* You choose how you behave. *You* have control over your responses and reactions. So take charge of yourself! I believe it is the way you deal with people and situations that creates a toxic environment. We have to deal with people who offend, insult, and challenge us every single day. It's up to us to learn how to deal with these situations in a way that works for us, not against us. I am a proponent of bucking up and not running. That's why I embrace solutions and believe saying "So-and-so is toxic" or "Company X is toxic" is the ultimate bad excuse. The word *toxic* gives you an easy way out, and I say reject it. This is based on my experience dealing with all sorts

of people and environments. There are bad people, and you should stay away from them. There are bad places, and you shouldn't go near them. *Toxic,* however, is something you create through your reactions. There is bad and there is good in this world. You will never be in a situation where you are surrounded only by or working only with your dearest friends and perfect people. That's not reality. I don't love every person I have worked with on *Bar Rescue*. Some of the owners I have met weren't nice people. But I can't let that stand in my way of doing a good job and helping the businesses and the people who depend on them for their livelihoods.

3. *Learn from the past but don't live there.* Do not let past mistakes define your future. Don't dwell on what happened yesterday; make the most of today. These are not clichés. You can't change the past and you can't predict the future, but you can decide to do some forward thinking today. You can learn a new skill today. You can pay your bills today. What can you do right now to put yourself in a better place tomorrow?

4. *Get out of the constant information loop.* It's great to be informed, but world events are beyond your control. The news can often be disheartening—and frankly, the best way to make positive change in the world and create that ripple effect many leaders talk about is by turning off the TV or Internet and getting out to make your business, your family, and yourself better. I am not saying you should ignore the world and local news events, but because of social media and the constant barrage of information that comes through every electronic device in our possession, we allow ourselves to be flooded with material that is not helping us. Spend fifteen minutes at most at the beginning and the end of each day on

current events. If you want to dig deeper into a particular subject, you know I am all for learning. However, don't drown in news you can do little or nothing about.

5. *Engage your community.* When you get out of your own head and into your community, meeting people and lending a helping hand, it's a lot harder to dwell on perceived slights that happen "to" you. The bonus is that community involvement often puts you in touch with people who can help and inspire you. Plus you will have less time to dwell on perceived problems. One of the greatest things I have done recently was to join the board of directors of St. Jude's Ranch for Children in Nevada. Not only is it a terrific organization that helps transform the lives of abused and at-risk children, young adults, and families, but it has also allowed me to connect with many families I would not have otherwise met in my new home state and get to know my amazing fellow board members. It has given me a new and important mission.

6. *Question your assumptions.* Actively question negative assumptions about your situation. Be consciously proactive and solution oriented as opposed to reactive to negative events or conditions. Think of your circumstance not as an obstacle but as an *asset.* Successful, productive people are masters at making obstacles into resources. If you are having a difficult time with a colleague at work, or if you notice that sales have been slow, or if you keep being turned down for jobs, what are these situations telling you? What are the ways a particular circumstance is an advantage? Is your problematic colleague offering clues to departmental troubles that could be solved by changing procedures? Write them down. What are ways this circumstance could present opportunities? If sales have

been slow, is it a chance to reevaluate your inventory and make changes to your buying strategy? How can you make a *no* into a *yes*? If you keep being passed over for new opportunities, perhaps it's time to update your skills or revise your résumé.

Derrick Coleman became deaf when he was three years old. Now he's an NFL fullback, currently with the Atlanta Falcons. In a great Duracell commercial, he explains how his obstacles became an asset. "I was picked on and picked last," he says. "Coaches didn't know how to talk to me. They gave up on me. Told me I should just quit. They didn't call my name. Told me it was over. But I've been deaf since I was three, so I didn't listen."[3] What an incredible gift that he could not hear the criticism from the people around him! His deafness has continued to be an asset on the field, because the crowd noise is not a distraction for him, as it can be for other, hearing players. This was especially crucial when he played for the Seahawks, because the Seattle stadium is considered one of the loudest in the NFL. Although deafness seems like it would be a huge disadvantage for an athlete, it turns out to have some important advantages.

Consider too that if a circumstance is an issue for you, it is probably troublesome for other people as well. Some of the most profitable businesses come from solving big problems. On-demand transportation services like Uber and Lyft have solved the problem many people have of not having a car or not being able to drive. Both companies were started by individuals who recognized an obstacle (no ride, dude) and figured out a way around it (a car shows up and takes you where you need to go for an affordable fee). Amazon made online shopping a breeze and continues to innovate in that arena. The company is big now, but one guy with a few employees started it. How can solving your problem be turned into a solution not just for you but also for thousands, millions, and perhaps billions of other people?

Location, Location, Location

One circumstance excuse I hear a lot from people is that they work or live in a lousy location—and so can't make their businesses or lives better because they're stuck in that place.

If you really think that your location is the problem, you have to do one of two things: move your location or make the location work for you. I've seen businesses in less than desirable locations do very well. The hole-in-the-wall that people go out of their way to visit, passing numerous other places on their way, has something going for it that makes location almost immaterial. Convenience is secondary to experience, and anyone who suggests otherwise is wrong.

Half a million people go to Orlando, the middle of nowhere, to visit Disney World on any given day. They stand on line in 100-degree heat for half an hour, pay exorbitant prices for a soda, but yet they have fun, and they do it all over again whenever the chance arises. If it is an amazing boutique, bar, restaurant, miniature golf course—whatever is compelling—then people will come. So the trick is to make your place compelling.

Charlie Alexander, who owns MoonRunners Saloon, had to deal with the reality of being in a forgotten part of Garner, outside of Raleigh, North Carolina. "We are located in an area where no one really goes anymore. Even though MoonRunners is a destination restaurant, it still does not bring in sufficient numbers to the location," he says. Charlie noticed that on Saturdays and Sundays the restaurant's sales were declining. He thought that maybe it was because his customers were busy enjoying the massive street fairs and open-air concerts that took place in downtown Raleigh on the weekends. He decided to use this insight to his advantage. "We added a food truck and catering to generate additional revenue and customers," he says. "We have a presence at these weekend events."

Charlie also sends the food truck to the most popular office buildings to provide high-quality eight- to ten-dollar meals to workers. "It's not the roach coach going from construction site to construction site," says Charlie. His truck does that during the day, and in the evenings, he partners with craft breweries that don't serve food. "We set up in their parking lot, which is another source of revenue and exposure. We are now in the breweries rotation of food trucks."

MoonRunners also does catering. Not the white-linen-type wedding catering, but a more casual format, such as backyard weddings, and organization events where the restaurant can provide box lunches. Even if people don't stop to eat, MoonRunners benefits from marketing collateral—impressions from the exposure in places where many people gather. "Between food truck and catering revenues, by end of 2017 we made an additional twenty to twenty-five percent in sales, and when we maximize what the food truck can do, we expect to see a thirty-five to forty percent increase in sales," says Charlie. Location is really not an excuse.

Think about turning your location's faults into its funky assets. I took over a restaurant in Dallas, Texas, several years ago. It had been in the same family for fifty years and the children had taken it over from their parents. The restaurant had become invisible in its location—plenty of people drove by, but they were on their way to someplace else. The restaurant was no longer a destination. We were brought in to renovate and update the property.

The restaurant was open while we did the work because the family was frugal and did not want to lose customers or revenue while the renovations were happening.

As part of the renovations, we painted the outside of the property. The painters came one day and primed the building with a special epoxy primer that happened to be bright pink. They were supposed to come back to put on the final coat, but it rained for several weeks so their work was postponed. Curiously, during that time when the restaurant was pink, revenues went up 225 percent. People came in and said, "Oh, I never noticed this place before, even though I have been driving by for ten years." What I learned from that experience is very important: the location was bad for the restaurant only because the restaurant blended in with its surroundings. Texas is beige and flat. The restaurant was beige. Once it was pink, all of a sudden it had the greatest location in the Lone Star State! (And we did paint it eventually, but we kept it a shade of pink.)

You *Can* Find Good People

"I can't find good people." This is one of the most annoying "That's just the way it is" excuses I hear from business owners.

My response: If you can't find the right people, then how the hell do your competitors find them? That's a perfect example of turning an objection into a question. Then answer the question. Maybe they have really good incentive programs. Perhaps your competitors have great scheduling apps that satisfy both part-time workers' need for free time on particular days and coverage for the business when it needs it. Ask the next natural question, which is, why don't good people work for me? Maybe it's because you are unprofessional and therefore have a bad reputation. If that's the issue, we can do something about it.

Maybe you have good people working for you, but you don't train them properly, and you don't give them feedback or manage them well. Maybe these good people are dying to come out of their shells, but you keep them stuck through lack of communication, bad scheduling, and lack of training.

Other reasons you might not have the best staff is because you pay less than your competitors or offer fewer benefits. Even in a buyer's market for jobs, these things still matter a great deal to people who seek work. Maybe it's time to do a competitive analysis of your business. What salaries do your competitors pay? How do they manage workers? Do they offer management training? Some of this information is easy to find out, other pieces may take a bit more work. You can start by talking to other owners or managers, joining business groups in your community and networking, talking to your own employees, and talking to workers at other companies.

The secret to building a successful team is looking beyond superficial elements, including an applicant's cover letter and résumé, to find the right personality for your needs. Choosing a candidate with a winning personality, connections, and skills helps to ensure you will have an employee who does his or her part to help your business succeed. Once you find someone with the right personality for the job, you can teach her how to work in your business.

Here is my view about teaching versus training. Training is behavior modification, and that happens when you are a child. If you do not look in my eyes when you meet me as an adult, it is impossible to change that behavior. If you have low energy or you are impatient, I can't change those things. I don't train people—I teach the right people for me how to work in my business. A person with a great personality and no experience can be taught how to work in a business within three days. Personality is money. To that end, remember the following when hiring:

* *Personality:* I cannot emphasize this enough—the key to hiring customer-facing employees is personality, not skill set. If a person's personality and interpersonal skills seem right, then is past experience even relevant? It's easier to teach someone procedures, duties, and specifications than to teach him to change his personality. Look for employees who demonstrate empathy, curiosity, grit, and collaborative tendencies. These types of employees are guaranteed to be intrinsically motivated and their hard work will definitely be a plus for your business.
* *Connections:* An employee with numerous solid connections to potential customers they could bring in, or employees you could hire, is priceless. When you harness the talent and energy that is in your combined network, you will be able to expand your reach and achieve your business objectives in a relatively efficient manner.
* *Curiosity:* In *Cat's Cradle,* Kurt Vonnegut wrote, "New knowledge is the most valuable commodity on earth. The more truth we have to work with, the richer we become." Hire people who can demonstrate an ability to learn, are flexible, and are curious about new information and ideas.

Bullshit Buster: Mark Itkin

Highly respected and regarded as one of the architects of the modern television syndication and nonscripted "reality" television models, Mark Itkin, an agent and show packager at WME, is responsible for bringing many popular and influential shows to the small screen, including *The Real World, Deal or No Deal, Extreme Makeover: Home Edition, Project Runway, The People's Court, The Ricki Lake Show,* and *American Gladiators.*

Mark was also a pioneer in identifying international programming that could be successfully adapted to American TV, including *Big Brother, Fear Factor,* and *Hell's Kitchen.* In short, Mark is the guy who can come up with an idea, find the right performers and production companies to make the show, pitch new concepts and ideas to networks, and make it all work. The popularity and profitability of reality TV are really because of Mark Itkin.

Mark is also a business partner of mine and one of my best friends. When I started to develop *Bar Rescue* I wrote up a brief about the show, which was originally called *On the Rocks.* I then met with Michael Braverman, a manager for entertainers and my first adviser in the television business. One of his jobs was to introduce me to industry people, and one of the people he wanted me to meet was Mark Itkin. "You have to meet Mark. He is the god of unscripted TV," he said. Today, about 70 percent of all shows are unscripted, and most of them went through Mark's hands at some point.

I tried to talk to Mark for two years but he would not return my phone calls. I e-mailed him, called, did whatever I could to meet him. It was frustrating. By this time *Bar Rescue* was in production and on the air. I had moved to another agency and things were moving along—the show was doing well in the ratings and we were being renewed. Out of the blue, two years into the show, I received a phone call from, of all people, Mark Itkin! This was a big deal—he finally noticed me. I went to the WME building to meet him in his beautiful corner office. Within minutes we hit it off and were talking like old friends. Mark represented me for one and a half years, up until his retirement. We still collaborate on projects even today. Mark's tenacity and ability to put disparate pieces together to create cohesive entertainment continues to amaze me.

When Mark started in the mailroom at the William Morris Agency (WME's predecessor), unscripted television was considered a "low-rent area," even though people like Oprah, Mark Goodson, and Merv Griffin had done very well and become quite wealthy from this kind of programming. "Most of the other people in the mailroom wanted to be actors' agents, writers' agents, movie agents, or work on prime-time drama or comedy—these were the areas that had cachet and respect," says Mark. "I didn't want to be like everyone else." However, he points out that one person before him who was packaging game and other daytime TV shows was Mike Ovitz, cofounder of the talent agency CAA and a huge player in the movie business.

"I had done a dissertation on daytime TV at UCLA. I knew it and watched it. I grew up as a middle-class kid where there was no snobbery, and I could watch everything. I really had very middle-class tastes, I was not a snob, and I got a feel when something could work or had the elements or had a cool title. When I thought about it, it made sense to work in daytime, which eventually morphed into prime-time reality programming. I was the first guy to do it. None of the other agents were doing it because it just wasn't considered cool," Mark says. He consciously chose a path that at the time did not have a great deal of respect in the industry, nor a lot of notice from higher-ups. For some people, that "circumstance" would have been a difficult one to traverse; it wasn't exactly a clear path to success and recognition. Mark didn't care.

"No one really understood what I did and few really knew about this kind of TV or what it could be, so they let me do my thing," he says. "I built the nonscripted department completely under the radar. I started accumulating various people in the arena of nonscripted TV, and eventually became the go-to guy in that because I planted the flag early on."

Another reason why Mark was able to take his less-than-glamorous circumstances (or so they were considered at the time) and make them so successful was that he took the programming seriously. "If I had a feeling in my gut that an idea or personality was exciting, then it was really worth spending some time on. I didn't want the buyer to ruin it, so I would look for the right people to produce it so that wouldn't happen." He also looked for overseas programming that could work in the American market. "I would look through boxes full of tapes of shows from clients such as John DeMole for anything with potential. Most of it was garbage, but ten percent was worth looking at. One show from Belgium was basically two teams of people who had to do these amazing stunts. For example, someone put on a uniform that protected him and let an angry German shepherd bite him while he ran from one spot to another. That show became *Fear Factor*."

Mark was able to make such a success out of an overlooked part of the industry because of his knowledge base. Growing up, he watched TV, and he studied it in school, but he also made an effort to understand the history of television and why people like certain shows. He advises anyone who may feel their career circumstances are limited to educate themselves. The more you know, the more options you have.

Don't assume the circumstances you are in can't lead to something hugely influential and lucrative. Mark's story proves that you can succeed by flipping the script on what you think of as an obstacle and making it an advantage. Today, Mark is a legend because he took that route.

Bullshit Buster: Christine King, Medical Exercise Specialist

Christine King is the founder and CEO of Your Best Fit, Inc. She started her own company after a horrific, life-altering Jet Ski accident that left her paralyzed and nearly killed her.

Christine was vice president of a video production company and training for a Miss Fitness USA competition. On a summer weekend in New England, she was Jet Skiing with some friends when they hit a wave, and she was thrown twenty feet in the air before landing back on the Jet Ski in a seated position.

When Christine opened her eyes and looked down at her legs, she says they "looked like two ropes that had been twisted, and I could not undo them." At that moment, she saw the whole rest of her life in a wheelchair.

Her friends surrounded her, and together they swam her back to shore as they were about two hundred feet out in the water. From there, Christine was put on a very slim wooden stretcher and loaded onto the back of a pickup truck, then slowly driven to the waiting ambulance, which could not drive onto the sandy beach. At the hospital, she finally got up the courage to ask a technician, "Did I break my back?" It was a devastating moment because she could tell by the look in his eyes that the answer was yes.

The local hospital could not handle her injuries, so Christine was put in a medevac and brought to Rhode Island Hospital, where she was taken into the trauma unit. "Ten to fifteen doctors surrounded me, trying to decide the best course of action. I was twenty-six years old," she recalls.

Despite the devastating news about her back and legs, Christine felt like she was in a good place. "My career was going well, and I read a lot of business books, and success books, so I had many good things in my head. I am a Christian, so I could lean on that too. I'm half Italian and half Irish, so I am thick headed. I went home too early, but I was in the gym on Monday after going home on Friday in a full body cast. I would exercise anything that would move. Little by little I started to get things back. My therapy was eight hours a day. I would not accept the fact that I was not going to walk again."

After twenty years in the fitness business, Christina says that if you can move any part of your body, build on that movement. Over time she got rid of the braces and the canes, which she credits to being in great shape before her accident. Her journey inspired her to leave the video production company and start helping other people change their lives through fitness. "I want to show people how fitness can help them too. I became certified as a personal trainer, and through the hardships of my physical and personal life, I kept building my personal training company and moving forward, and still do it to this day."

Today Christine and her team work with everyone, from children to adults, and from athletes to people with injuries. "We are going to get you to do what you can do," she says. "Many people come to us not believing they can get better. Menopausal women say, 'I will never lose weight.' You can do it and you do not have to kill yourself to do it. You have to make it realistic; it can be done. You can still do what you want to do; if you are paralyzed from the waist down, you can move your upper body and you can become the best chef. You can't always listen to the doctors; I have seen people do miraculous things with their legs after the time limit set by doctors. Don't give up."

Christine turned what could have been a devastating circumstance into the impetus to do something very different with her life. An accident could have become a whopper of an excuse, but Christine chose to let her circumstances become her inspiration.

Bullshit Buster: Ed Meek

In 1983 Ed Meek was running his publishing company, Oxford Publishing, which put out a handful of national trade magazines on topics ranging from hospitality to satellite communications to health care. That year, he bought *Nightclub & Bar* magazine from Ole Miss graduate Laurie Heavy after the publication ran into some financial troubles.

As a natural entrepreneur and "idea man," Ed thought that a small trade show would benefit bar owners as well, so he put together a few educational speakers who were successful and knowledgeable about the bar business, and quickly organized an event. I met Ed around this time, when I was a young guy in the bar business. He asked me to speak at the convention—and it's grown larger than either of us would have thought. Today the event is described as the largest food and beverage trade show in the Western Hemisphere, and Ed was named one of the top one hundred most influential people in the trade-show industry by *Tradeshow Week* magazine. Now held in Las Vegas, the convention draws about thirty-two thousand buyers and more than two thousand exhibitors.

When he started this event, Ed didn't know anything about the bar and restaurant business—and, coming from the Bible Belt and a very conservative, teetotaler background, he wasn't going to begin learning about it now. He went into a business he knew nothing about, and one whose entire product line he avoided. For many, that could prove to be a negative circumstance, but for Ed it was a winning strategy.

"I was publishing magazines in niche markets and in subjects I didn't know anything about," he says. Instead, Ed learned that you could make an idea happen by going to the experts. "My mother would have rolled over in her grave had she known about the nightclub business I had entered. However, I saw a great opportunity, a great need that I could fill by hiring the right people, so I never let my personal feelings enter into it," says Ed. Together we, and others whom he guided in the business aspects, put together a product that grew and grew. I would keynote every show because I could draw a crowd like no one else.

Ed also says that no matter the circumstances, you have to persevere and believe in yourself. "My success is based on finding ideas and staying with them until I make them happen, despite circumstances. I taught for thirty-six years, and I always noticed it was not the straight-A students who have done well in life; it was the average-grade ladies and men in the back of the class who were motivated and stayed with their ideas no matter what happened."

There are two books that Ed says changed his life and helped him to overcome any difficult circumstances and reach his goals. The first is *Success Through a Positive Mental Attitude* by Napoleon Hill and W. Clement Stone. "It made me believe in the power of positive thinking because I've seen it work in my own life so many times. If you train yourself to think about ideas, you can make them happen. I write ideas down all the time, when I am traveling, waiting in line, everywhere. I keep a notebook with me to jot down ideas that later become businesses, and I credit a lot of my success with that book. Among the ideas was my observation during a trip somewhere that my small town didn't have a convenience store. When I got back home, I set upon creating a convenience store in my town, and that store still exists," says Ed.

The second book Ed recommends is *How to Get Control of Your Time and Your Life* by Alan Lakein. "Good entrepreneurs by nature can be terrible organizers, so you have to force yourself to give time and attention to what is important, and that little book helped me do that. It's a short, simple book, but what great advice. Lakein says don't ever touch a piece of paper more than once. If the paper is worth acting on, act on it now, and if it isn't worth anything, get rid of it. Another strategy Lakein offers is to simply make a to-do list of what you will do tomorrow, and put the most important thing on top. Do that before you do anything else on the list. What you find is that you may never do the Cs on the list, but if you do the Cs, you will *never* get to the As and Bs—the really important stuff."

You're going to be confronted with negative and positive events and side effects outside your control throughout life and work. You have the wherewithal to deal with them. There is never going to be a perfect time or a perfect situation to make your business or life work, so don't wait for them to come along.

With *Bar Rescue,* I've met many bar owners who refuse to adapt to circumstances, and that is why they fail. The key to handling circumstances, whatever they are, is being able to adapt to whatever is going on around you in ways that profit you. You have to learn to be agile and adaptable, and to be able to adjust to the inevitable and the unexpected. Understand that you exist to serve customers and clients; the customers don't exist to make business convenient or easy for you. Things go wrong, circumstances do change, accidents happen, and you will make mistakes. Expect them. Be ready for them.

Adapt or die!

DBY To-Do List

* Take a second—or third—look.
* Take the existing environment and adapt to it so you can serve existing stakeholders and attract new ones. See unchangeable circumstances not as obstacles that allow you to give up but as opportunities for growth. Successful, excuse-free people work *with* what they have.
* Come on, get happy!
* If you have a tendency to see all or most barriers as impenetrable to your success and well-being, you have to do a little work to change that. If you're not naturally optimistic, you can practice being optimistic. Begin by not putting so much stock into what other people think. Don't use toxic people and situations as an excuse for toxic reactions. You choose how you behave, react, and respond. Learn from the past but don't live there.

Don't get caught up in the constant social media information loop. Engage your community and become part of it. Flip the script. Actively question your negative assumptions about your situation.

* Deal with existing conditions; don't be defined by them.
* Bottom line: every "problem" has a solution. If you really think that your location is the problem, you have to do one of two things: move your location or make the location work for you. If you stay, the trick is to make your place compelling. Likewise, the secret to building a successful team is looking beyond superficial elements, including an applicant's cover letter and résumé, to find the right personality for your needs.

Chapter 5

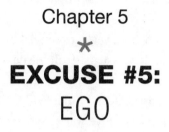

EXCUSE #5:
EGO

"Avoid having your ego so close to your position that when your position falls, your ego goes with it."

**—Colin Powell, American statesman
and retired four-star general**

Excuses Based on Internal Beliefs and Bad Habits

Our egos are more than happy to provide us with self-definitions that help us avoid responsibility for our inactions or actions. Our egos also allow us to indulge in behaviors we should avoid; we give in to temptation because we want to feel good in the short term. We want immediate gratification, even if in the end it does not serve us. The ego wants to be both fed and shielded from harm. What we believe about ourselves as far as what we can and can't do is often our biggest obstacle. It's time for us to get over ourselves!

I know that ego excuses usually have very little to do with reality, but they are comfortable and easy to believe. We go along with these excuses to protect our egos from possible disappointment and embarrassment. Psychologists call the device we use to distance ourselves from potential unpleasantness a defense mechanism. According to psychologist Anjhula Mya Singh Bais, Ph.D., "Making excuses is an effective way to either self-rationalize or manipulate an external situation or persons. Instead of dealing with old wounds and hurts from childhood and life, the ego subconsciously blocks out any information that triggers and does not support, bolster or promote its well-being."[1] The problem is that when we let our egos get in the way of action we also distance ourselves from success, prosperity, progress, and realizing our full potential.

In order to get rid of negative self-talk and an ego that doesn't want you to get out of your comfort zone, you need to believe in an alternative opinion of yourself through *action*. Hillel the Elder, the leader of the Jewish Supreme Court in Israel in the early part of the first century C.E., said, "If I am not for myself, who will be for me?" And "If not now, when?" Words to live by.

After speaking at a Budweiser convention in Las Vegas in 2010, an audience member suggested that I would be great on television. I had never considered being on television but this encouragement gave me the impetus I needed to write up a treatment, or short description, for a show idea I had. I showed it to producers at Paramount and was told, "Jon, you will never be on television. Hosts are young and good-looking. You are too old and

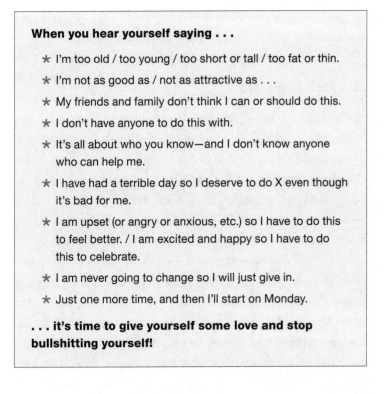

When you hear yourself saying . . .

* ✳ I'm too old / too young / too short or tall / too fat or thin.
* ✳ I'm not as good as / not as attractive as . . .
* ✳ My friends and family don't think I can or should do this.
* ✳ I don't have anyone to do this with.
* ✳ It's all about who you know—and I don't know anyone who can help me.
* ✳ I have had a terrible day so I deserve to do X even though it's bad for me.
* ✳ I am upset (or angry or anxious, etc.) so I have to do this to feel better. / I am excited and happy so I have to do this to celebrate.
* ✳ I am never going to change so I will just give in.
* ✳ Just one more time, and then I'll start on Monday.

. . . it's time to give yourself some love and stop bullshitting yourself!

not good-looking enough. Don't waste your time." Rejection turned into inspiration. Instead of walking away with my tail between my legs, I got my pit bull on. Getting on TV became a vendetta for me. I used my own money to shoot a three-minute sizzle reel in Hermosa Beach, California, which pretty much showed me screaming and yelling at bar owners. I brought it to three production companies. They all wanted it and sent me offers within a week. In my case, I used my ego to get my ambition into overdrive and fulfill my goal of developing and starring in a very high-quality and informative unscripted TV show.

Get rid of the story you've made up about yourself or that you have allowed other people to foster and find the truth.

It's Not Too Late

We often make ego excuses regarding our age,[2] which is too bad. I believe that *nothing* is too late until your heart stops beating. If you are reading this, you are alive—so it's not too late. You have the ability to change things, challenge the status quo, beat the odds, and start something new. Yes, there is always going to be someone younger, richer, thinner, smarter, and more charming than you out there. That's the way the world works.

Face it, I match no television executive's typical description of what a perfect host or even reality character looks, talks, or walks like. Here I am, defying some imaginary odds, the central character in a show that I created. *Bar Rescue* premiered in 2011 and, as of this writing, is going into its sixth season with more than 150 episodes and more than 70 million viewers on a television network primarily directed at young males. An astounding 77 million people watched season four! I just finished shooting a pilot for ABC, my first network project, and we are now finalizing a talk show. We are shown in five continents and on more than five thousand channels and dubbed in Portuguese, Italian, and Spanish. We are negotiating even more shows, taking us close to two hundred episodes, which is unheard of in the reality-TV space. *Bar Rescue*'s success is past anything I could have imagined. How the hell did that happen?

One reason the show is such a hit is because I refused to think about or take seriously the conventional idea of what a TV host should be. I just did not let the fact that I did not fit the existing criteria deter me. There's no law that says a TV host has to be twenty-five and a former bodybuilder. Media—and all business— like to repeat success, so they tend to piggyback on what works and are afraid to get out of that comfort zone. That's why you see copycats of so many successful products. This doesn't mean you can't do something completely different and get your stakeholders, whether suppliers or customers, out of their comfort zones.

The producers and I knew we had something good, *I* knew I could pull it off, and I projected that confidence. You are not too "anything" (old, young, pretty, plain, whatever) to try something *and* succeed. There are other unlikely television people who have made it in an industry that seems obsessed with youth and beauty. Ina Garten, host of *Barefoot Contessa* on the Food Network, is not tall, thin, or young—yet she has one of the most successful franchises in the food world. She was fifty-four when her show debuted in 2002.

Or take actor Reed Birney, born in 1954, who won Best Featured Actor in a Play at the 2016 Tony Awards for his role in *The Humans*. During his acceptance speech, Birney said something remarkable: "The last thing I want to say is I've been an actor for almost forty-two years, which I cannot believe I am saying. All thirty-five of them were pretty bad and that's a lot of them and I just couldn't get anything going. So the last eight have been great, but the thing that was always great wherever I was, whatever level I was on, were the amazing people I got to work with, almost all of them were hilarious and talented and full of passion and joy and they loved putting on plays and telling stories. They always have been and are still the best part of what I do and I am so grateful to all of you and I love sharing the planet with all of you."[3]

Here is someone who had been toughing it out in a difficult

industry for forty-two years, never throwing in the towel. Birney finally got a great part and won a Tony Award after many years of pounding the pavement and being rejected. Yet he's tremendously grateful despite the difficult road he traveled.

Harry Bernstein published a short story back in 1934, when he was 24 years old. Yet it was not until 2007, when he was 96 years old, that he published a memoir, *The Invisible Wall,* about growing up Jewish and poor in a northern English mill town.

During the 1950s Mr. Bernstein, who died in 2011 at 101, tried to make a living as a writer, and did sell work to *the New York Daily News, Popular Mechanics,* and *Family Circle.* Eventually he ended up editing *Home of Tomorrow,* a construction trade magazine. He published a novel in 1981, but it sold poorly.

"The first 25 years of my life are something I would rather forget, but the contrary has taken place," he told *The Guardian* in 2007. "The older I get the more alive those years have become." He published two more books, one a follow-up memoir, published in 2008, and a third in 2009. Reflecting on his path, Harry said, "If I had not lived until I was 90, I would not have been able to write this book. It just could not have been done even when I was 10 years younger. I wasn't ready. God knows what other potentials lurk in other people, if we could only keep them alive well into their 90s."[4]

Next time you're tempted to use age as an excuse, think of me and think of Harry Bernstein.

Be Who You Are

Not only can we talk ourselves out of something because we feel "too old," we can also tell ourselves lies about other attributes, like our appearance, and how being "too" something else will stop us from doing something we want to do.

At forty-five, Brett Singer decided to finally take a crack at professional acting after years of thinking he was too tall to be an actor. "I had gone to the High School of Performing Arts, and I acted, produced, and directed in college, and even started my own theater company," he says. "When I got out of college I could have started auditioning for things, but out of fear I just didn't. I thought at six feet three inches I was too tall to be an actor." Brett wasn't wrong—truth be told, most actors are small in stature. Tom Cruise, Daniel Radcliffe, Al Pacino, James McAvoy, and many other leading men are well under six feet tall. When someone who is very tall is working with someone much shorter it is hard to shoot scenes unless you want to have an obvious difference in characters' heights. Even so, height is still not a reason not to try acting. Rules exist to be broken.

Instead, Brett went into theater administration, and from there he found his way into the publicity business. "I had my own theater publicity business, enough to support my family while my wife was in law school, but the interest in acting never went away. I had young children, and I was not in a good financial position nor did I think of myself as actor," says Brett. Eventually Brett transitioned from PR to journalism, as writing was something he also liked to do. Still, acting nagged at his soul. He didn't feel ready to give up his day job and wondered if he had enough time to go on countless auditions and still earn enough money to provide for his family. Now not only did he think he might be too tall—he also thought he might be too old! "The fact that people like Michael Caine or Samuel L. Jackson keep working into old age inspired me."

When he realized he could take the time to go on auditions,

and acting didn't necessarily have to bring in income, he decided to listen to his heart and give acting a go. What really changed his mind? "You start to get older and you realize you will not live forever. You start to listen less to your ego and more to what you really want to do—or you should. I also wanted my kids to learn that, through me." The fact is, the height factor (and the age factor) was really all in Brett's head. A friend from college had started a theater company in San Francisco, and he called Brett wondering if he would be willing to do a reading. "I said sure. Not only was it an incredibly fun script, but when I did the reading, everybody there said, 'Oh, my God, you're really good!' That doesn't hurt. Despite the fact that I never allowed myself to think of acting as an option, I also have a sure-I'll-try-that attitude about most things." After he did that reading, he was asked to do another reading, and then was asked to do a monologue by a former classmate who is now a producer.

"I took a class to brush up on my training, and I also signed up for *Backstage* magazine, which lists almost all open auditions." Once you pay for a subscription, you can go to backstage.com and upload your résumé and head shot. That way you can click on auditions and apply right from home. "It's like Candy Crush for actors," says Brett. The subscription had already paid for itself by the time we talked, as it had helped Brett land several paying acting gigs.

It took nerve and willingness to open up to rejection, which is a big part of auditioning. "You go out and stand there and read for someone and then they say no, we do not want you. It's still a lot of fun. The only way to do it is to actually try doing it so I don't mind the rejection. Rejection doesn't do anything to my ego, because I know I'm not going to get every part. No one does. I'm old enough to know how lucky I am."

Every week, after an episode of *Bar Rescue,* someone insults my actions or appearance on social media. Those insults never bother me nor can I take them personally. Allowing rejection to impact me would kill my ability to be on television just as it would damage anyone's feeling of self-worth—but only if you let it bother you.

Five Ways to Flip Your Script

The personality that cannot change is really the personality that refuses to change. When you believe your self is flawed in such a way that it stops you from pursuing your dreams, that's a self-pity play. The self-pity play denies you self-respect, and if you *really* believe trash talk about yourself, you should close your business tomorrow because you will *never* be successful with that attitude. *Your* attitude—you own it.

However, if you know you're lying to yourself, and you're indulging in feeling sorry for yourself, you have a chance. Self-pity is just a trap, but it's one you can get out of. When you feel this way about yourself, it's generally masking another problem—likely another one of the excuses in this book. Identify the underlying issue that leads to pathetic and immobilizing self-pity. You may feel you don't know enough to run a business or continue working in your role at your job. While it may be true that another job may suit you better, feeling sorry for yourself doesn't change anything. You need to make it your business to learn about the things you don't know about. If you're worried about money, read the money chapter. If you're worried about your employees, pick up a book on management.

Wrapping yourself in self-pity spoils any chance of being able to see new possibilities as they appear. Agreeing to live with regrets ensures only that they'll still be with you tomorrow. Why would you want that? I've seen this syndrome so many times, especially in the tough arenas of hospitality and retail, that I just had to figure out something uncomplicated people could do to change their own attitudes.

The following strategies force you to pause and question your beliefs.

IMPLEMENT A ZERO TOLERANCE POLICY FOR YOUR OWN DARK FEELINGS

You have to consciously stop the pity narrative that is running endlessly in your brain. Because you have free will, you can stop yourself from thinking dark thoughts. Visualize throwing away negative feelings, or literally do it—write down dark emotions on a piece of paper and then crumple it up or set it on fire (safely, of course). List in your mind or on paper everything that is going right in your life. This helps you see that your negative thoughts are out of whack with the reality of your life. Gratitude helps us become more appreciative of what we have. Every day recommit to stop joining in when the pity party comes calling. It's not going to be easy; the ingrained patterns in your brain feel comfortable even when they encourage self-pity.

PRACTICE BEING POSITIVE

Healthy self-esteem prevents you from being caught up in self-pity and is a defense against criticism that can often stop your progress. I am not asking you to ignore what could be constructive criticism. I am asking you to respond to it in sensible ways that help you move forward. Regular exercise, even twenty to thirty minutes a day, is one way. Eating better and drinking less are essential. Take time to do some community service, and get to know or reach out to other people in your industry. Try something that is out of your natural comfort zone. Learn solid financial management. Learn that you don't need to spend money to be happy, and that the things you own don't define your worth. Finally, get a little gratitude in your life. No matter how little you *think* you have, you have many things to be grateful for—so start recognizing them. All of these things build self-confidence and get you out of your head.

ASK YOURSELF IF IT'S REALLY TRUE—DO YOU HAVE PROOF?

When you say or think something about yourself, take a moment to ask yourself if it is really true or if it is just a story you tell yourself—or someone else's story about you that you choose to believe. If something is true, does it make a difference in terms of what you're trying to accomplish? For example, if you say, "I'm too overweight to work in sales," is that because you've tried to get a job in sales and been turned down specifically because you are overweight—or is it all in your head? If it *is* true, weight is something you can work on, but it should not stop you from seeking or getting a job. Instead of telling yourself you can't get a job because of your size, start telling yourself you can get a job because of your personality, qualifications, and talent. Changing negative self-talk to positive ideas that are true works over time.

Steve Buscemi is an incredible actor with amazing credits to his name. He's not exactly George Clooney in the looks department, but that doesn't make a difference at all in terms of his success. What if he had told himself, "I am not as traditionally handsome as many leading men in Hollywood, so I should give up on an acting career"? Did it mean he couldn't be a successful actor? No, absolutely not.

Professional cartoonist Robin Ha grew up in Seoul, South Korea, and stayed out of the kitchen, leaving that task to her mother. "I always thought cooking was something I could never do. [Korean food] looks really complicated," Ha told NBC News. However, a few years after graduating from the Rhode Island School of Design, Ha moved to Bay Ridge, Brooklyn, where there were no Korean restaurants. She asked her mother for simple recipes and slowly began to make Korean food in her modest Brooklyn kitchen. The more recipes she successfully made, the more she understood that not only could she cook, she was becoming very good at it. After becoming beyond proficient in Korean cooking, her friends took note and started asking her for tips and recipes. As a result, in 2014 she started a weekly comic on Tumblr, "Banchan in Two Pages," to explain how to make basic Korean side dishes. An editor from Ten Speed Press noticed its popularity and asked Ha if she would be interested in turning the material into a cookbook. In July 2016, the then-thirty-five-year-old cartoonist published *Cook Korean!* "I haven't been educated in culinary school or in a kitchen," she says. Nevertheless, Ha stopped listening to the idea—her own—that she couldn't cook. Because there was no proof she couldn't cook, she went ahead and tried it out of necessity. Look where it took her.

What do you tell yourself that holds you back? Is it true? Do you have proof? When you buy a house, you don't just look at the front of it and make a decision. Even professional house flippers who are buying quickly try to look in the windows and walk the perimeter of the property before making an offer. Most people know it is wise to look at the front of the house, the sides, the back, the basement, and the roof and examine all the rooms before proceeding with a buy. Are you giving yourself the same courtesy of investigating your assumptions?

DON'T COMPARE YOURSELF WITH OTHERS

Comparing your progress, wealth, appearance, social standing, and other markers of "success" with people in your peer group is human nature. It's tough not to do; I get that. Comparing certain aspects of your life, such as your retirement savings or your cholesterol levels, with members of your demographic can even serve as a benchmark—something you can learn from. It's not the final word on your own situation but it gives you some information you can use to make positive changes.

We get into trouble when we use comparisons to deny ourselves the right to take action. The "I'm not good enough" ego excuse is based on looking at others and deciding they are better and their levels of achievement are somehow unreachable for you. You don't have to try particularly hard to find someone who looks like they are doing better than you and, as a consequence, to feel bad about it. A 2005 study published in the *Quarterly Journal of Economics* called "Neighbors as Negatives: Relative Earnings and Well-Being" found that "higher earnings of neighbors were associated with lower levels of self-reported happiness."[5]

In other words, people felt bad about themselves if they thought their neighbors made more money than they did. Erzo F. P. Luttmer, the author of the study and an associate professor of economics at Dartmouth College, told the *New York Times* that neighbors "influence what you think is a normal lifestyle, and you struggle to keep up." This struggle can distract you from things you could and should be doing to make your life better by directing you toward things that you think will impress the neighbors— who probably don't care or even think all that much about you. You may be avoiding challenging yourself to do better because you feel defeated.

Ultimately, comparisons put the focus on the wrong person, and that is the person or group you are comparing yourself with. The focus should be on you. The self-criticism that results leads to a distorted sense of reality and the inability to learn from mistakes, according to a study by Michael Inzlicht, Ph.D., a psychologist at the University of Toronto, and his colleagues. I have worked with more than one bar and small business owner who failed because they had "comparison paralysis"—they were so defeated by how their neighbors were doing, they just stopped trying to be competitive and closed up shop.

Give yourself some credit when comparison-based self-doubt creeps into your mind. When you're tempted to start comparing yourself with those you perceive as doing better, remember that it's just a perception because you never have the whole picture of another person's life and business. You can also make note of some of the great things you have going for you. University of Colorado psychologist Joshua Correll, Ph.D., found that people who identify things they value and "own," such as their families, laughter, creative pursuits, and so on, reduce their anxiety and increase their ability to solve problems and improve upon real flaws.[6] Focus on your own successes!

Find inspiration through authentic knowledge seeking. Looking at what successful people do is worthwhile only if the information gleaned is instructive and useful. Find out what the most successful people in your field do, and learn what you can emulate to achieve your own goals. Peers, industry leaders, well-known success stories, people you know personally, and those whom you know about only because of their notoriety—all are great resources as inspirational examples. Walt Disney has long been an inspiration for me, and even though he is long gone, his legacy and his business acumen are a constant source of insight.

Compare with yourself; compete with yourself. Look at where you were five years or twelve months ago. What has improved? What can you do better? What's the best you've ever done at something? How can you beat your own record? Positive self-tracking is a great way to stay motivated and on task.

Also, get some fresh air. A change of scenery, even if it's a walk around the block, can help clear your head of negative self-talk and comparison mode. According to a study done by researchers at the University of Michigan, nature walks are associated with improved well-being and lower perceived stress. Researchers found that people who walked reduced the effects of stress in their lives and improved their emotional and psychological well-being. I know when I am out driving my tour bus, something I love to do, the stress of the day disappears as I take in the sights and sounds of the open road.

GIVE IT TIME

Don't slow down your own progress or the progress of others just because you don't see any immediate gratification down the road. Successful and productive people see the greater reward of a successful company and want to play a part in building something cool that will benefit them down the line. Three core skills go right to the heart of the "Time is running out" thought and the "There's nothing in it for me anyway" syndrome. Three things absolutely necessary for success are the ability to plan for the future; delaying gratification; and something called commonweal orientation, or a general concern for the well-being of your community.

You can see entire groups of people who are unable to get out of a cycle of poverty and failure because they cannot think of anything except their current needs and are unable to wait for and work toward something better. Instead of saving up for something they might actually *need* to succeed, like a car or a college education, they buy expensive sneakers or a fancy cell phone instead.

The famous marshmallow study shows this clearly. In the study, researchers told children that they could have a marshmallow right now, but if they waited for a defined period of time, they could get two marshmallows. Some children gobbled up the marshmallow and others waited patiently so they could have twice the fun. In a follow-up to the study, researchers found that those who had been able to wait for a second marshmallow succeeded better in school, in their careers, and in life than those who could not wait.

Cancel Your Subscription to Negativity

Negativity is an infectious disease that has dire consequences. The eye rollers, complainers, and whiners with short fuses and quick tempers wear people out with their temper tantrums and constant grievances. All-or-nothing thinking—when you think anything less than perfection or anything less than everything you want is failure—is unproductive. The person who focuses only on the negative aspects of any situation denies reality. Negative thinkers who project their own bad feelings onto others and misinterpret what other people say ruin productive relationships. Negative thinking can also have bad outcomes for your health and well-being. People who get into a cycle of chronic "Why me?" thinking are at a higher risk for late-onset depression and a decline in cognitive function, according to a study from the University of New South Wales. Another study linked high levels of cynicism later in life to a greater risk of dementia, and a research project that looked at data from almost one hundred thousand women found that the most pessimistic participants were more likely to have heart disease than positive-thinking women. Additionally, the more negative thinkers had a higher chance of dying over the study period compared with the more positive group. According to a 2014 hostility study, unfriendly people had a higher risk of stroke than the friendlier study subjects.

An addiction to negativity isn't good for your career either. In my experience, managers consider negative employees a drain on morale and productivity. Eventually, they get rid of them before the damage they do gets too severe. Employees have no respect for negative managers or owners, and will either quit or stop paying attention and allow their work to slide and their responsibilities to take a backseat to other concerns. Unfortunately, negativity is a common habit among the failing business owners I meet, which is why I talk so much about changing someone's thinking first, before changing anything about his business. Too many people automatically see the bad before the good in any situation; they gossip, whine, and complain.

At one bar I tried to rescue in Las Vegas, the owner could not kick his habit of being cynical and angry. He abused his employees and customers, and his attitude killed the ambience of what could have been a fun bar in a great location. The owner refused to show up on the opening night of his renovated and rebranded bar, and, in fact, refused to even open the bar after we left. His own negativity was ruinous. He gutted the place and planned to renovate and reopen the bar, but it never happened.

Negative thinking also kills creativity. A "That idea will never work" atmosphere discourages innovation that could help a struggling company or one in a challenging business create new products, develop more efficient ways of doing business, or simply survive and thrive. When a workplace becomes adversarial, people do not feel the need to share ideas.

Harvey ran a bookstore in a mid-size midwestern city. For a brick-and-mortar bookstore to remain successful today, it has to compete not only with online sellers but with other brick-and-mortar retail that offers interesting experiences for shoppers as well.

Harvey's employees, who loved books and also wanted to keep their jobs and serve their community, which was attracting more and more young people and millennials, had loads of ideas about how to draw new customers to the store and keep them coming back. One employee, Hannah, recommended installing inexpensively built walls that would create cozy and quiet spaces in which to dip into books and feel cocooned combined with more open spaces where people could sit together and hear authors and others talk about a variety of subjects. This event space in the middle of the store could also host poetry slams, movie nights, wine or food tastings, and other events to draw both new and current buyers into the shop. This idea was proven, as it had worked in other bookstores that were staying in business *and* busy.

Another employee, Frank, had ideas about how to make the exterior of the store buzz with activities, including outdoor book-stalls and sidewalk tables in nice weather. He wanted to add eye-catching displays at the entryway. Frank thought Harvey should embrace what was happening in the technology side of the book business and celebrate it by installing a self-printing kiosk in the store so buyers could order books the store did not have room to shelve. A rare and old book section would encourage a different kind of browser and buyer.

These were all great ideas that would not cost much money. Harvey dismissed all of them and insisted he was going to do business as he always had. After a few months, both Hannah and Frank left the store and went to work for someone else who welcomed their ideas. A few months later Harvey was forced to have a going-out-of-business sale and closed the store. Tragic—and completely avoidable.

The Ego and Temptation

"Just one more time won't hurt me." This egocentric lie is so tempting and self-indulgent, it's hard to say no to it. Try to, because "just once" can turn into forever very quickly, and that can screw up your chances of doing what needs to be done. "Just once" is the flip side of procrastination. Instead of putting off doing something that helps us, we do something that hurts us. It's an easy trap to fall into because while "just one more time" may be technically true, very few of us can actually hold to that promise.

Sure, one piece of cake at the wedding won't hurt your blood sugar or waistline. However, one piece of cake often turns into cookies, crackers, candy, soda, and pie with whipped cream on top for the rest of the week, month, and year. One helping of chips, one missed trip to the gym, one night spent vegging out in front of a *Bar Rescue* marathon. "Just once" can turn into too many broken promises. Your brain knows it can get away with this excuse next time too, and the time after that, and so on, until you are giving yourself insulin shots and using the motorized shopping cart at Walmart.

When I talk about temptation, I am talking about the kinds of behaviors that allow us to get up in the morning and function, but don't allow us to reach our full potential. I am not qualified to talk about serious addictions to substances—that's a different matter, and if you have a problem with drugs or alcohol, you need to deal with it before you think about anything else. When I'm talking about limiting behaviors, I think about the ski bum who can't resist one more trip down the mountain but never gets his shit together to actually act on his dream of having a ski shop; the habitual gossip who never gains anyone's trust, so she is forever passed over for promotions and lucrative assignments; the slacker who consistently blows off deadlines in favor of taking vacations and, as a result, stays stuck in the same job for years. If you recognize some of your own traits in these examples, I can help you, by helping to change the way you *think*.

Quit for a Higher Purpose

Unfortunately, many of us don't realize that the thing we can't resist has become a negative habitual behavior that hurts us, even if it gives us an emotional boost in the short term. Breaking bad habits is twofold. First, you have to become self-aware enough to understand what behaviors are damaging your credibility and limiting your ability to get things done, and second, you have to find a reason beyond yourself to stop doing them. It's time to both look in the mirror and be honest with yourself. What behaviors are holding you back and who else is being affected by them? If you don't break these habits for yourself, do it for your family and your friends. Considering the negative impacts on your own future as well as on that of your loved ones may help you to resist temptation.

Take people who are trying to quit smoking. Smoking can have a deleterious effect on your success. Aside from the physical damage it does to your internal organs, it can cause premature deterioration of your physical appearance, adversely affect fertility, and can also affect your job prospects. According to a study in *JAMA Internal Medicine,* smokers remain unemployed longer than nonsmokers, and they earn substantially less when they are hired. To help determine whether smoking may actually prevent people from getting jobs, the researchers surveyed 131 unemployed smokers and 120 unemployed nonsmokers with follow-up surveys six and twelve months later. After a year, only 27 percent of smokers had found jobs, while 56 percent of nonsmokers had been hired and were working. The smokers who had found jobs earned, on average, five dollars less an hour than nonsmokers. Still, those reasons may not be enough to get you to toss the pack in the trash.

Before my daughter was born I smoked several packs of cigarettes a day. In 1985, a couple of weeks before her due date, I was sitting in my office hacking and coughing. It was disgusting. I started to think, *Is this the kind of behavior I want to model in front of my daughter?* I put that cigarette out and never smoked again.

Right after my daughter was born, I bought a novelty item, a cigarette and a match in a little glass tube that was labeled "In an emergency" on the front. I carried the tube in my pocket for two months. Anytime I thought about smoking I would take it out and look at it, and look at a picture of my daughter. *Which one is more important?* I'd ask myself, and then I'd wind up putting the tube back in my pocket.

My discipline and willpower are not perfect. Yet the inspiration to quit smoking came from a higher purpose; I had to do it for my daughter. It was more important to my ego, my sense of self, to do something right for my daughter (and me) than it was to continue to enjoy the sensation smoking gave me. Ultimately, I did not want her to grow up seeing me smoke. I use this higher-reason thinking on *Bar Rescue* often. If you don't want to stop doing something that is hurting you (and your business and your family) for your own sake, then do it for your kids, your spouse, your future, and their future. This generally gets people to pay attention. When we can find a higher calling, we can achieve a higher purpose. While I could never manage to quit smoking for myself, I *could* do it for my daughter.

Mike is a terrific guy who lives in my neighborhood. In almost every area of his life—as a father, an entrepreneur, a coach to his son's baseball team, a sibling, and a son—Mike is a champ. But he's also a guy who had been trying to reverse his type 2 diabetes for years. He took a ton of medication but his diabetes stuck around. He tried to cut back on sugar and other trigger foods, but he had a tough time doing it. It was always "Oh I'll just have one piece of bread with lunch," or "An ice cream on the weekend won't hurt." Of course, the ice cream and the bread and the snacks and the candy were *all* hurting Mike.

One day, Mike had a wake-up call. He met a man who had kidney disease, in this case as a direct result of his diabetes. Mike had young children at home—he could not risk becoming incapacitated or dying, leaving his wife all alone to care for their family. So Mike became A Person Who Doesn't. In his case, he was A Person Who Doesn't Eat Processed Carbs or Sugar. Until he realized his children might have to grow up without him, Mike wasn't interested in really trying to end his negative food habits. The change in his diet actually reversed his type 2 diabetes, and today he is off the meds. He feels better, is more engaged with his family and his job, and is optimistic every day.

Help Yourself

Compulsive, damaging behaviors are found in people from every demographic and in all industries. "I can't resist" is a lousy excuse for not getting yourself together. I believe you can change. I believe you can turn a page and replace a bad habit with a good one.

BE ACCOUNTABLE

Mentors, or the buddy system, is one of the best ways to keep your own promise to beat bad habits. The well-known Framingham Heart Study found that people were much more successful at quitting smoking when it was done with other people, and when friends and family members were around to keep quitters responsible. There are people in my life who are important and help me not only to work through problems but also to stay focused on what's important.

Writer and producer Keven Undergaro and his partner,

broadcaster Maria Menounos (whom you met earlier), are two of my best friends. My wife, Nicole, and I get together with them frequently to talk about business, our lives, television, and the media. We have so many things in common, as we are all in television and are constantly trying to come up with new media ventures. That means we can be great sounding boards for one another. That's really important. Friends and mentors whom you can talk to openly keep you honest. Mentors, as Keven and Maria are for me, should be able to tell you when you are doing something that's not working in your best interests.

Don't underestimate your family, especially your spouse or life partner, if you have one. Couples can sometimes shield each other from problems, but then we miss out on the benefit of the support we could give each other, and the honest insight into our behaviors and how they affect those around us. We have to pull those people more deeply into our lives. One of my greatest mentors is my wife. She may not know as much as I do about the hospitality business or the television business, but she knows *me* very well. She may be much younger than me, but her life experiences, combined with her understanding of how my mind works, give her a great perspective. Her advice and insights are extremely valuable to me. She will also tell me if my habits are getting in my way. That's a gift. Your greatest mentor may be right next to you on the couch—let that person in.

KEEP TRACK

Making note of your behavior is a great way to see patterns. When I rescue a bar it is easy for me, as an outsider and a professional, to see an owner or staff member's destructive patterns almost right away. However, when you're deep into your own bullshit, you can be blind to the times when you slip up and when you repeat behaviors in response to certain triggers. For instance, if waiting on line triggers your temper, you have to either find a way to avoid long lines or figure out something you can do as a distraction from the waiting, like reading something interesting on your smartphone, or even playing a digital game.

I also recommend getting a notepad to start keeping track of yourself. I suggest keeping a record for at least a week, but two would be even better, either at the end of each day or, if possible, while the behavior is happening. When do you engage in your negative habitual behavior? When you feel out of control (e.g., waiting on a long line)? When you're bored? Angry? Tired? Once you've done that you can look at your behavior and you will see patterns, I guarantee it. Once you understand when and why your bad habits get the better of you, you can take action to redirect your ego and your behaviors. Intellectually you may know that smoking is bad for your health, overeating can lead to chronic diseases, getting angry at store clerks doesn't make you feel better, and drinking and taking drugs can royally screw up your life. However, seeing it in writing has power.

Alexandra had a demanding and stressful job managing an international law firm in Manhattan. These kinds of firms are often open twenty-four hours a day. Not only did Alexandra manage the office during the four-p.m.-to-midnight shift, she was also in charge of the day and overnight managers. That meant she had to ensure that a team of lawyers in five countries were happy, the office ran smoothly, and the other managers had what they needed to do their shifts.

She medicated herself throughout her shift with food from

the local deli, the pastry cart, and the vending machines in the lobby of the building where the firm was located. In three years' time she was forty pounds overweight, diagnosed with sleep apnea, and completely exhausted all the time. Her job performance slipped, and the partners in the firm noticed, not to mention her two managers.

"The only person who had the nerve to confront me was the lead lawyer in the New York office," says Alexandra. He told me, 'Look, you have to figure out how to get back to your high-performance levels, otherwise we're going to have to either demote you or fire you.' The fact that he was so candid was a gift, because without that stern and serious warning, I just would have continued on my way down the sugar drain." Alexandra went to a cognitive behavior specialist and started keeping a food journal. She wrote down the times when she ate "extra food"—food that was not part of a meal. "I got so sick of writing, my hand hurt," she says. It didn't even take her a week to see that she was grabbing snacks four or five times a day while at work, and even more frequently when she was at home.

Alexandra noticed other patterns too: "I rarely wrote down the word *hunger*. In fact, I don't think I ever wrote it down. I usually wrote down *tired* or *anxious* as reasons for my eating."

Working with a therapist helped Alexandra come up with healthier alternatives to her behavior. "If I felt anxious and wanted to eat, I would stop and think about why I was anxious. If I needed help with work, I would ask for it instead of eating a doughnut." She also got her sleep apnea checked out and was given a CPAP machine, which she says really changed her life.

It took several months, but after about a year of cognitive therapy and changing her eating habits, Alexandra was down to her fighting weight and sleeping better. Her work performance went back to its previous stellar level. Once she started tracking her behavior—thanks to the intervention from that law firm partner—she was able to have control over her temptations. One of the other strategies that helped Alexandra get rid of her food thoughts was to say to herself—sometimes as a whisper and sometimes just in her mind—"I'm not interested in that anymore," or "I don't need that food." There were times when she had to say those phrases to herself hundreds of times a day. "But it worked," she says.

Bullshit Buster: Brad Bohannan

Brad Bohannan may be one of the most memorable bar owners who appeared on *Bar Rescue*. His bar, Spirits on Bourbon (formerly Turtle Bay), is now a huge draw for locals and tourists alike in New Orleans. Of all the *Bar Rescue* subjects, Brad has been the best marketer. He has taken what we did on the show and used it to create a huge platform; he out-markets everyone around him through events, public speaking, social media campaigns, and innovative products, and that it why he has been so successful.

Brad was able to make it in New Orleans despite being an outsider, which is rare. He moved to town as a newlywed, as his wife was finishing her undergraduate work at Louisiana State University. Throughout his own college career, he had worked at Marriott hotels.

Brad started as a doorman at a bar and restaurant, and subsequently worked his way up in a bar business on Bourbon Street in New Orleans. "When I was working, I was hustling. I tended bar, and then became the manager. I was very frugal and I worked every day, open to close." Eventually, Brad saved enough to put his wife through law school and help her open her own practice. He then had the opportunity to become a partner in a business on Bourbon Street with the people for whom he had been working. He took out a large business loan, and because of that he became millions of dollars in debt. This was a huge obligation, so the business that the loan was based on had to be a success in order to pay back the loan.

Then, in 2005, Hurricane Katrina hit. Brad was in Missouri during the storm, trying to figure out what would happen to the business. "I was in my brother's basement in Missouri, watching the city fall apart, thinking, *What do I do now? Am I going to work at Applebee's as a waiter?*" When he returned to New Orleans, Brad was able to fix the moderate damage done to the bar and open it right away. "We were the first business to reopen in the neighborhood," says Brad. "We were serving soldiers who had been called in to secure the area. We were the first business on Bourbon Street to have guests." Unfortunately, more trouble was on the horizon.

"The people I worked for and partnered with had become like parents to me," Brad says. "However, there was never a point where I didn't think it would go bad, because I had observed over time that all their relationships went bad. I knew that." Brad acknowledges that it was a risk to go into business with the couple, but his ego told him he could overcome the problems he had seen them have with other people. This is a common mistake. We often think we are the ones who can "change" a person—when ultimately people can change only themselves.

"They were having issues sharing the money with me, and then we had a fire in one of the bars," Brad says. That gave them an opportunity to get him out of the business. The partners went into litigation and Brad was happy with the settlement. He walked away from his first business with his freedom and its best manager, Steve Smith. Lesson learned.

After that, Brad opened a place on his own—in a space that was right across the street from the bar owned by his former partners. "It was very hard because of my relationships with the people I had worked so hard for and had been so successful with. They tried to stop me from building the bar, and tried to push me out with legal maneuverings that didn't work," he says. "When that happened all I could think about were ways to make them fail."

That thinking was a problem for Brad, and something we had to work on. He was hurt by what the couple had done to him, and instead of working on making his business a success he was working on finding ways to hurt their business. His ego was getting the better of him and his business prospects.

One day I took a walk with Brad down Bourbon Street and talked to him about this problem with his wounded ego. "Brad, the best revenge is being successful," I said. "You have to stop trying to hurt them, and focus on building your business and making it the most successful business it can be." Brad took that advice, shifting his focus from things he could not control, like other people's businesses, and got to work on his own success. We cleaned up the kitchen, and made sure the gumbo the bar was producing was made from fresh ingredients. We created a blue drink called "Resurrection," which has now become part of the destination status of the bar, meaning people come to the bar specifically to have that drink. A vintage barber chair in the main room is also a draw. Once Brad shifted his focus and started to work on his business, his revenues increased and the consistency and quality of his bar's products went way up.

I have yet to meet another bar owner who throws himself so totally into making his business work quite the way Brad does. He is always innovating, making improvements, maintaining consistency and quality, and looking for new ways to bring attention to his bars, whether it's through public and motivational speaking or through robust social media efforts. It's incredible to see someone take some basic tools and use them to his full advantage.

Bullshit Buster: Sean Al-Bawwab

I first encountered the St8 (pronounced "State") Pub in Englewood, Colorado, in the season seven premiere of *Bar Rescue*. The manager, Sean Al-Bawwab, had basically been handed the keys to the bar, along with the promise of a potential partnership if he could keep it running smoothly and pay the two-thousand-dollars-a-month rent. What an incredible opportunity for anyone who wants to get into the bar and hospitality business—a dream situation that doesn't come along very often.

Thirteen months into this dream venture, though, Sean had created a nightmare. Not a single rent payment had been made, the bar was diving into oblivion, and Sean, along with his friends, was drinking away the profits every night. When I came on the scene, Sean was thirty-five thousand dollars in debt. The owner gave Sean an ultimatum: in five weeks he had to pay all the money he owed, or he would take back the bar and find another manager.

At that point Sean was down to one employee, bartender Caitlin. His mother paid the rent on this thirty-three-year-old man's apartment and helped keep the bar "clean"—which isn't saying much because no matter how many times Pamela swept the floor, she couldn't keep up with the crud in the kitchen, behind the bar, and even in the bottles of liquor and the taps. Further, Sean's apathy and negativity created an unpleasant atmosphere that turned customers and former staffers against him. Even his friends had no respect for him.

Sean treated the bar like his own personal playground, and instead of being a prospective owner with a positive attitude, he got hammered every night, abused customers, called former employees names (which is why they quit and he had only one left), and staggered around the kitchen reheating contaminated food. Sean even proudly admitted to drinking more than any customer who had ever come into the place. He isn't an alcoholic; he just treated the bar like his personal man cave. Anyone who interfered with his fun got nothing but attitude from Sean.

The first order of business was to ensure that Sean was not drinking on the job. When he was sober he was a completely different person—responsible, friendly, and on the ball. Unfortunately, as soon as he got to the bar he started to drink, and he would be completely smashed before happy hour began for customers. He could barely stand up straight when five o'clock rolled around, which was stupid and irresponsible. Sean also had to learn gratitude and realize that having a bar owner who was willing to give him the bar if he succeeded in running it and a mother who wanted him to succeed were two advantages many people could only dream about.

I brought in a team of experts, as I usually do, and we developed a series of new restaurant items and drinks that would entice customers to the bar, which was fewer than ten miles from downtown Denver. We ramped up the bar's craft beer offerings and educated his new staff on how to sell the products to customers, whether they were knowledgeable about craft beer or neophytes. My experts taught them how to make great-tasting drinks and food in a clean bar and kitchen. We renamed the pub Downstairs Kitchen & Bar, and turned it into a bar version of the greatest man-cave basement joint you could dream of. Fun, modern, kitsch, and clean, Downstairs Kitchen & Bar suited the demographics of the area and played off the kind of place Sean wanted it to be—the ultimate cheesy but contemporary man cave. Mom Pamela agreed to be Sean's "buddy" and hold him accountable for his behavior and his drinking.

Today, Sean pays his rent steadily, and is paying back his debt to the bar's owner. He no longer drinks on the job, and he expects his friends to pay for what they order, just like any other customers. Sean has also tried hard to kick his addiction to negativity and apathy, which were the root causes of his failure to be a responsible manager.

Our egos can get in the way of so many opportunities. It's like a massive control panel directing how we interpret daily experiences. Our perceptions and reactions are then formed by those interpretations, whether it's through negative self-talk, inaction, or destructive habits. Our egos also want to protect us from hurt and defend against potential disappointment and failure. As a result, we impose limits on ourselves in terms of what we are willing to try and even what we are willing to think about others and ourselves.

To fight a powerful ego, remember: be aware of your biases and limits, ask for help when you need it, don't let other people determine how you feel, and always ask yourself if what you believe about your own abilities is really true.

Put your conscious mind in charge, not your ego!

DBY To-Do List

* Get past thinking you're "too" anything.
* I defied the odds of being on TV, Brett Singer defied the odds of being a tall actor, and Reed Birney defied the odds of spending his acting career going unrecognized by winning a Tony after forty-plus years in the business. Countless other people have defied the odds by changing from thinking they were "too [fill in the blank]" to realizing it was all in their heads. Harry Bernstein published a bestselling memoir at ninety-six years old. Be who you are, and let that shine!
* Flip your script.
* Self-pity is just a trap, but it's one you can get out of. Make it your business to implement a zero-tolerance policy for your own dark feelings and negative self-talk. Practice being positive and ask yourself if the things you believe about yourself are really true. Do you have proof? Probably not! If they are true, does it really make a difference? Stop comparing yourself with others. We get into trouble when we use comparisons to deny ourselves the right to take action. Focus on your own successes. Find inspiration through authentic knowledge seeking. Compete with yourself. Look at where you were five years or twelve months ago. What has improved? What can you do better? What's the best you've ever done at something? How can you beat your own record? Positive self-tracking is a great way to stay motivated and on task.

* Help yourself.
* *"Just one more time won't hurt me."* This egocentric lie is so tempting and self-indulgent, it's hard to say no to it. Start to be accountable for your own behavior. Get a buddy or mentor to help keep you on track. Write down your triggers and notice the patterns of your behavior so you can anticipate and change them.

Chapter 6

*

EXCUSE #6:
SCARCITY

"For those who do not live in fear of scarcity, life is unlimited."

—Jonathan Lockwood Huie, author,
trainer, and personal coach

Excuses Based on Lack of Funds or Resources, or Not Having "Enough"

"I don't have enough money or resources to succeed." People often cry the no-cash blues to me when they're trying to explain why they can't improve their business or start a new one, or even afford to take a coveted trip or buy a new car. However, when we sit down and really look at their situations, we find that their issues are usually caused by either a misallocation of their resources or not thinking correctly about their assets. I meet so many owners who do not have a clear picture of their financial status and assets that could be turned into cash if necessary. Bar owners have told me they couldn't afford to buy lemons, and then I stepped outside into their parking lots and saw an expensive sports car or other luxury vehicle parked in the owner's spot. No matter how well I have done in life, I never bought a car unless I could put 50 percent down.

You may be strapped for cash right now—and that can be genuinely painful. I've been there. There were times in my career when I had very little money or lost a great deal of money yet still had to provide for my family. I know from personal experience that there's no reason you need to be stuck in a cash-poor state forever. You can start or turn around a business, pay off a loan, and expand your horizons, even with very little. The key is to take an honest look at the way you choose to spend the money you do have or are taking in. You can start or improve a business with very little money, and that's what I will focus on in this chapter.

Don't sell tomorrow for today. Whether you are trying to start a business or working your tail off trying to make ends meet until your next office promotion, you can learn to use money wisely, save money, and make money work for you. If you need money for any reason—and this chapter focuses on those of you who would like to start a business either as a sideline or as a full-time gig—start by making better choices. You may have to sell your car and get a cheaper one. You may have to move to less-expensive digs. Costs can be cut without sacrificing quality. Debt can be paid off in reasonable ways, and innovation, product development, and marketing don't have to cost much, or anything, in the right environments and with the right mind-set.

When you hear yourself saying . . .

 ∗ I don't have the money to get started.

 ∗ There is no way I can reduce my expenses.

 ∗ I need to continue earning exactly what I earn now.

 ∗ I can't make any changes until I pay off my debt.

 ∗ I need more savings before I take a risk.

 ∗ I don't make enough money to put any aside.

 ∗ What if I can't make any money at it?

 ∗ I have no safety net.

 ∗ If I fail, I will be left with nothing.

. . . it's time to get over your scarcity excuses and stop bullshitting yourself!

Just Try It

Let's say you have a great idea for a service or a product, such as a smartphone-driven healthy-breakfast delivery service or a solar-powered fire pit, but no funds to create samples or prototypes. Sure, it would be nice to have a venture capitalist sweep in and hand you a wad of cash, or your aunt Betty to leave you her fortune, but that's probably not going to happen. *However, not having money is no excuse.* If you are confident that you have an idea for a business that solves a problem and that people will want, and even if you aren't 100 percent confident (who is?), don't let the money excuse derail you.

Start-up costs have decreased in recent years because of the availability of so many low- and no-cost tech solutions. Today, creating a professional-looking Web site is affordable and impressively easy to do. Social media allows you to advertise or distribute your work for virtually nothing. Smartphones make video production a breeze. Old-fashioned footwork, research, and person-to-person selling are still powerful tools when starting a business, and also cost nothing.

My grandfather gave me great advice. He said, "The size of your phone book is more important than the size of your check-book," because great relationships are much more valuable than money. Whom do you know? How can they help you? The people you know may even be your first customers.

When I learned about Kael Robinson I was impressed with her diligence and creativity. She started her company, Live Worldly LLC, with forty dollars and an instinct about how fashion trends form.[1] In 2007 a friend had given her a "wish bracelet." As you put the cloth bracelet on, you were supposed to make three wishes. Six months after receiving the bracelet, Kael, then twenty-seven, lost her job at a public-relations firm. At the time she was also working a few hours a week as a lacrosse coach at a Denver, Colorado, high school. After she was let go she took a planned trip to Argentina, where she noticed many young women wearing wish bracelets similar to the one she had. The observation of their extreme popularity got her thinking.

Once home, she bought one hundred of the bracelets for $40 from a South American wholesaler. She wore five of them to a lacrosse practice, and offered them to her team for $2.50 each. They quickly sold out so she bought another hundred pieces. The lacrosse team was the perfect demographic because Kael knew fashion trends often start at the teenage level and then move into the larger culture. It wasn't long before Kael had more orders than she could fill.

She ordered a thousand more from her wholesaler and raised the price per unit to $5. Next, she started to cold-call local boutiques to see if they would sell her product on consignment. Several agreed. Over time, retailers throughout the state and beyond began to place orders. By the summer of 2008, Kael had earned enough to pay for a professional Web site and logo for her company. She hired a publicist friend who helped her write and distribute press releases to major magazines catering to her demographic, young and trend-conscious women. *CosmoGIRL!* gave her company its first national attention with a short blurb.

Kael used the *CosmoGIRL!* clip to contact higher-end retailers, including Barneys New York, Fred Segal, and Kitson. She sent each of them a copy of the article along with fifty bracelets in a glass bowl ready for display. The stores sold out of the samples within a week and ordered more.

The following winter, Kael asked foreign buyers if they had an interest in distributing the bracelets and many said yes. Within a short time, she expanded her catalog to include other products from around the globe, the unifying principle being some kind of special meaning or cultural significance. She also started an adventure travel company that helps people immerse themselves in the culture of places like India, Bali, and Kenya. As of this writing, her products are available in more than five hundred stores worldwide. According to Kael, Live Worldly has made a profit since its inception. It's not a major profit, and Kael lives frugally, watches expenditures, and works on developing her business every day. However, she did not have to go back to office work and managed to make a living doing something she finds exciting and engaging—and worthwhile.

Kael made an observation—wish bracelets were popular

overseas and her American lacrosse players seemed interested in them too—and turned that and forty bucks into an international business.

When I had the idea for *Bar Rescue* I didn't have the kind of funding that producing a television show or series required, and I was not prepared to put a great deal of my own money into the project. That didn't stop me. Writing a brief explanation of the show's concept and the main players in it cost me nothing but my time. I hired a friend who was a cameraman and a lighting man for about two thousand dollars to create the sizzle reel. The first title of the show was *On the Rocks,* but in testing we realized people thought the show was about bad marriages so we nixed the name. It became *Bar Rehab* and then *Bars on the Brink.* Finally, we landed on *Bar Rescue.* We sent the package to a production company with a pitch letter, and the people there liked it enough to propose the show to Spike—and the network loved it.

I had an idea for a television show so I put together a package to show producers. Kael had an idea to sell bracelets she had seen on a trip to Argentina. Neither of us, and countless other people who start businesses, agonized over scarcity of funds or resources. We didn't worry too much or question our ability to pay for what we wanted to do. We just started doing it. Our passion was more important than how we'd find the money to get going, our curiosity and interest the driving force behind us. Those things do not require a big bank account. If you want to do something, what can you start doing about it *today*? Whom do you know who can help? Your first customers could very well be your neighbors, friends, and colleagues.

Remember too that if you are passionate about a business idea and serious about getting it started, lack of funds is quite likely to be a temporary condition. The adage "Do what you love and the money will follow" has been proven true many times over. It can be true for you too.

Create a Plan

When I say create a plan, I don't mean a complex business plan in the formal sense of the word. Most entrepreneurs don't actually have to write an extensive business plan unless they are seeking substantial funding from a venture capitalist or a bank—and for many of you that is not going to be the case. Microloans and small business loans don't require you to roll out forty-plus-page proposals. However, you do have to put your ideas down on paper.

Everything I do I start on paper: every promotional idea, every market analysis, and every new creative endeavor. I look at it, digest it overnight, and reread and revise the next day. I see what's missing and what doesn't need to be there. Putting things on paper makes ideas concrete. It is worth the time and effort. I want you to create a plan of action, and then systematically implement the plan. Frankly, putting an idea down on paper, organizing its moving parts, is the only way you will really know how much, if any, money you need. Whether you're starting a side business and keeping your day job or going all in and starting from scratch, here's how to get started:

1. *Make your idea specific.* This needn't be complicated. Write down your idea and describe it.
   * Determine the goal and mission of your company.
   * Why are you different?

* Who is your audience? Who is going to buy your product or service?
* Why will your buyer want your product or service?
* How will you be paid?

2. *Give it a name.* Naming your business makes it official. Once you have a name you can

* Secure a domain name for a Web site (build a free Web site using WordPress to get started or use one of the low-cost e-commerce Web-building sites).
* Register the business in your state as an LLC or an S corporation (whichever is appropriate). LLCs have few paperwork requirements and offer some real benefits to a small business, such as personal asset protection and tax advantages. For instance, an LLC can enter into contracts and obtain a loan that will not have an impact on its members' personal assets. Profits and losses of an S corp pass through to the corporation's owner, which allows you to avoid double taxation. Discuss these options with a qualified accountant—what may sound scary may actually have many benefits for your small business and you.
* Have business cards made (there are printing companies that provide free business cards in exchange for a small line of advertising on the back of the card).
* Set up a PayPal account.

3. *Give yourself a deadline.* Thirty to sixty days is a good amount of time for a small start-up to put its basic infrastructure in place, particularly if it is a service or a business you can run from remote locations or from home.

* If you need a brick-and-mortar location, you can find a property to rent within thirty to sixty days, including all the paperwork necessary for utilities.
* A basic Web site can be set up within one month.

4. *Broadcast it.* Don't be a nuisance, but give friends, family, colleagues, and other contacts a heads-up that you're starting a business. This is your network. They may be able to offer help and support.
* Send out an e-mail blast to your network.
* Introduce yourself to colleagues in your area.
* Let your social media networks know what you're up to.
* Introduce yourself to local businesses and business organizations (chamber of commerce, etc.) that could offer support.

5. *Work on your business every day.* Devote a part of each day to developing your ideas, finding new networks, and creating profitable connections.
* Identify and reach out to new contacts.
* Research conferences and educational opportunities that will help evolve your business.
* Meet with colleagues.
* Find a mentor or mentoring programs for entrepreneurs.

6. *Get creative about funding.* There are some types of businesses, particularly those that require brick-and-mortar locations, inventory, and employees—such as retail businesses, bars and restaurants, auto repair shops, health care, and some types of services, like law firms and real estate—that require funding. You do need capital to rent space, buy equipment

and inventory, and hire help. Again, being short on cash is not an excuse to forgo starting such a business. You may have to hold off while you raise the necessary funds, but that's not impossible. Here's how:

* Get a line of credit. There is nothing unusual about a start-up using or having access to a line of credit. Many major and local banks and credit institutions offer credit at favorable interest rates that are specifically designed to allow for growth in the early stages of a business. However, you have to have collateral or assets to get a loan, and a proven ability to pay back any loan you take. If you do not have income or collateral to support a loan, you may need a partner who does or who can invest in your business. I caution you not to overspend— you still have to live and work frugally. When you use credit you have to pay it back. It's debt like any other debt—don't get under water.

* Consider using a business incubator. These are organizations that help you grow your business by providing access to office space, management training, angel investors, and contact with economic development groups. One of the greatest incubators, Innevation (yes, with an *e*), is located in Las Vegas. It is owned by Rob Roy, CEO and founder of Switch, a data-storage technology company and one of the most socially conscious companies I know of. While Innevation does not refer to itself as an incubator, it offers many of the services that incubators provide, such as office space, conference rooms, and networking opportunities, and out of those opportunities, relationships that lead to funding in investments may develop. SCORE is another great resource that provides mentors, advisers, and business consultants to small

businesses and entrepreneurs. The National Business Incubation Association has more than fourteen hundred members in the United States alone. It has a search engine and a directory of state business incubation associations. Other sources for finding the right incubator for your business are state and local economic development offices, and local SBA (Small Business Administration) offices. Some business incubators are sponsored by colleges and universities, so if you are near or in a college town, check them out as well.

* Social media–inspired crowdfunding platforms have changed the way individuals and small businesses can raise money for projects. GoFundMe, Kickstarter, Indiegogo, Kiva, and many others allow individuals to invest small to large amounts of money in return for a variety of types of future buy-ins or stakes.

Get Ready to Work Hard and Get Creative

You have to get in the trenches and make your business happen, especially if you don't have huge funding to hire staff and outsource. The only way to generate revenue is to roll up your sleeves and get to work. Most of the time this means wearing many hats. In the beginning, you have to be willing to knock on doors, work the booth at trade shows yourself, negotiate your own deals, answer the phones, make your own coffee and lunch, and sweep the floors at night. In short, you might have to be salesperson, lawyer, marketing manager, secretary, cook, and janitor all in the same day. You'll also have to be smart and creative about money and the things that cost money, like inventory and staff. Below are some tips.

GO WITH THE CASH FLOW

Making more money isn't simply about generating revenue; it also means choosing how best to reinvest in your business once you have earned some money. You have to be ruthless about how you spend your time and money. If your budget is restricted, be strategic about spending. I advise moving from front to back. To prioritize, think: Invest in the guest. That means if you are on a limited budget, spend the most money on things that guests or clients can see, taste, smell, and experience. Make certain everything a guest or customer touches is as perfect as it can be. For instance, if you are selling a product, buy the best display cases you can afford. If you have an actual brick-and-mortar location, ensure that the exterior and interior are inviting, clean, and attractive. If your office will host clients, make sure the waiting and meeting rooms are spotless, comfortable, and uncluttered. If I need new flooring in the front of my business, I am going to buy the best I can afford. If I need a new piece of back-office equipment, such as a printer, I will certainly buy one, but it may not be brand-new and it may not look the best—because the customer can't see it.

Here are some smart ways to reinvest in your business:

* *Accountant:* Without good accounting, a business can get into trouble pretty easily. Even if you are starting to figure out your business and revenues are growing, you can still run out of money faster than you might think—and go out of business because you ran out of money. That's what happens to many bars—they get to the point where they are making a little money, but because of mismanagement (overspending, bad planning)

it runs out and they can't pay the rent. If they had an accounting system in place that took into account future expenses and could predict fluctuations in cash flow, they might have made it over the hump. Entrepreneurs tend to look at accounting last when they should look at it first. An accountant can help you determine how much you need and when you'll need it, and put a system in place to make sure you hit those targets. Unless you really enjoy doing tax paperwork, such as payroll and tax payments and filings, hire an accounting firm to help make sure you're in compliance and paying bills. The cost is tax deductible. You might be able to do the job adequately, but your time is probably better spent on things you can actually monetize, like acquiring new customers and keeping the ones you have happy. If you screw up on the financial side of things, you could do a lot of damage to your business. In addition, automate as much accounting and bill-paying functions as possible, so that you know they are being taken care of without worry.

* *Customers:* Customers equal income. Too many small business owners have no structure in place for knowing who their potential customers or clients are, and how they think, what they want, where they live, and why they seek out goods or services. Owners have to learn about getting new customers, customer frequency, and how much customers spend. In my experience, you have to generate at least 20 percent new business every month to mitigate business you lose every month, which is about 20 percent on average and sometimes more. Unfortunately, not enough business owners understand how they can get new customers, get those customers to come more

often, and then get them to spend more when they come. I have used response cards, which customers fill out on the spot to tell you how you are doing. One problem with these cards is that they offer limited information. People fill them out for two reasons: if they had a really great time or if they had a really bad time. The people who had a mediocre time don't fill out the cards; they just never come back. You have to understand your customers and potential customers to understand how to attract them to your business. There are now programs that help you keep track of how your customer retention programs work, including a few good ones I recommend below. Find the right one for you because there are always new sales and consumer tracking programs entering the market.

* Contactually helps you keep notes on people in your life and reminds you to stay in touch with them.

* AWeber is an e-mail marketing tool that captures leads and makes sales offers. It lets you know who opened your e-mails and when, so you have a good idea of audience engagement.

* Infusionsoft offers sales automation, link tracking, and shopping cart and affiliate management. It's not as inexpensive as other options, but it may save you a couple of hours a day, so it *could* be worth it if you have numerous contacts that you want to stay in touch with.

* *Knowledge:* As I discussed earlier in the book, there are many free sources of information and education. However, there may come a point where you want to meet new colleagues, network, and do in-depth learning on a particular subject. Perhaps you want to get certain certifications that will help you build a higher-end client base or build your reputation or credibility. That education is worth paying for.

HIRE PEOPLE YOU KNOW AND TRUST

If you have any budget at all for extra help, it is a good idea to hire people with whom you have worked before and whom you have complete confidence in to carry out their responsibilities. That way, you won't have to spend too much time training, and when you need to travel or be away from the business for any reason and for any amount of time, you know you'll have trusted staff to hold down the fort while you're gone. Be cautious about family members. Communicate clearly about roles and expectations. Write rules and procedures down in an employee handbook and let people know what you expect of them. If friends tell you they will work for free, be careful and consider paying them something. You have to make it clear that you will still treat them like paid employees. Will they want to work for free if you call them at two a.m. with a crisis?

EXPLOIT SOCIAL MEDIA

A friend and colleague of mine were talking about social media and how hard it is to monetize "followers" and "likes." Social media can also be a time suck, which is a genuine waste of your money. Understand what social media can do for your specific business, and then focus on platforms that give you real ROI (return on investment). I won't stop using social media, and right now I use Twitter and Facebook to connect with fans, but spending time on it is not how I use my most valuable hours of the day. Social media is always available, so you can work on it during off hours, in the evening, and during downtime. Here is my Social Media 101 primer:

* *Snapchat:* 60 percent of Snapchat users in the United States are under the age of 24, and more than 100 million users consume thirty minutes of content on the site every day. That means it can be a worthwhile place for businesses that target millennials. If you create video content of any kind, Snapchat provides a free marketing opportunity to distribute all sorts of information, including interviews, demonstrations, new collections, performances, and so on. I know of bars and restaurants that use the app to send coupons for special discounts on cocktails and meals.

* *Facebook:* The social media powerhouse skews older than other similar sites. American women and men between the ages of 25 and 54 make up 32 percent and 29 percent of Facebook users, respectively. A whopping 44 percent of these people check Facebook several times a day. By contrast, only 9 percent of users are between the ages of 18 and 24. If your target customer is over 24, create a company page on the site so that you have a presence there. You can provide contact information, information about new products or releases, and you can engage with customers, observe comments, and interact. If you have a business it should have a Facebook page. My Facebook Bar Rescue page (https://www.facebook.com/BarRescue) allows me to engage with fans, learn what they are thinking, and share news about upcoming programs and events.

* *Instagram:* This visual site has 500 million users, and nearly 60 percent check their accounts daily. Instagram has changed the way its users see information, so it's no longer chronological but based on a proprietary system that responds to how users interact with the site. Instagram is valuable only as a supplement to your brand-building efforts and not as a marketing

or sales tool. It's fantastic for posting images from your business. For hospitality businesses, it's a natural resource for posting delectable images of creative cocktails and scrumptious dishes to engage and tempt customers. People who sell anything that has an aesthetic component, such as crafts, art, antiques, jewelry, or fashion, should exploit this platform.

* *Pinterest:* If you have a large female-based clientele, Pinterest is worth investing time in, because 42 percent of women online are Pinterest users (34 percent are between the ages of 18 and 29, and 28 percent are between the ages of 30 and 49). If you are in a food, fashion, art, home decor, antique, pet, or artisan/craft business, Pinterest is a great resource for reaching interested people. It also has a new Pinterest "buy" button, so you can help customers buy your products from the site.

Turn It Around

When I was the general manager of a chain of Holiday Inns in the Midwest, I was faced with the responsibility of improving old, outdated restaurants that were attached to the hotels. Turnover was massive at this chain, and every time a new general manager came in he would order new plates or furniture, but never with any consistency. As a result, there was no cohesive, consistent theme in any property. The only unifying message the restaurants sent was "We're old, dated, and tired."

The hotel franchisor's director of quality control came to see me shortly after I started the job. As we toured the properties in the group, I wasn't surprised when he said they were substandard. He was right. They were also losing money. As he was a major player in the hierarchy of the hotel chain, I had to take his criticism seriously. He could pull my sign down and close the restaurants. What was I going to do? I had no money! My budget was limited to what Holiday Inn said I could spend, and it wasn't much.

"You have to make things in each restaurant match," the director told me. I looked at my budget and clearly there was no money to update six hotel restaurants. Instead of whining to him and ranting about how broke we were and how impossible it was to make the restaurants look consistent, my team rented a U-Haul, and then drove it around the six properties and mixed up everything we had even more than it already was, including the dishes and silverware. On purpose.

Once I was done, every item was boldly and obviously mismatched in every way—tables, chairs, glassware, flatware—so it appeared *obviously deliberate*. It was great! I created a concept based on a rural feel, including calling the restaurants Village Marketplace, where nothing matched on purpose. We built old-fashioned-looking carts out of cheap, rough-hewn pine and old wagon wheels, and filled them with hay and fruit. It cost me about four hundred dollars for each restaurant, which included the U-Haul rental, materials and labor to build the carts, cleaning, and the time it took to do the switching of furnishings and tableware and the setup.

The quality control director came back after the "renovation" was complete and was stopped in his tracks. "You son of a bitch," he said. "You did it and I can't argue with it." The moral of the story is that I took a liability where nothing matched and turned it into an asset where nothing matched. When guests came into the restaurants they could immediately identify the theme and anticipate a friendly, country-style, casual dining experience, and that's exactly what we gave them: simple comfort food in a charming environment. Employees were happier because they felt they worked for a company that had a distinct mission and vision, so productivity increased. Customers loved the charm of the restaurants and revenues went up.

Doug, a young East Coast entrepreneur, founded a clothing and accessories manufacturing firm in 2005. The company is premised around the idea of cutting-edge custom designs for millennial businesses and their audiences. He saw room for a company that could create beautiful promotional items, like T-shirts and wearable accessories, that were more stylish and contemporary than what was available. It has done work for theatrical productions, television shows, YouTube personalities, and local brick-and-mortar businesses, including food, wine, and clothing stores. Doug's original investment was about five hundred dollars of his own money to create T-shirt, cap, and jacket samples to show prospective customers. Two major orders, one from a local tech company that wanted branded clothing for employees and another from a small chain of local cheese and gourmet-food stores, gave him the funding he needed to start his business, which he did with just four employees—friends working together. "We all did everything, from packing T-shirts and caps into plastic bags to keeping track of inventory and making deliveries," says Doug.

The company grew, and by 2009, Doug had gone from four to thirty-five employees. Even so, revenues were not growing fast enough and there was an undercurrent of anxiety among employees about the sustainability of the business. Some loyal clients complained about late orders. There was a lack of focus among employees and everyone came to Doug with the smallest question or decision. Doug says, "We were often working at cross-purposes. We did not share a common vision for right now or for the future. When I lost a longtime client to an overseas manufacturer, I became very concerned."

He also noticed that people on the creative side were butting heads with people in sales, marketing, and accounting more often—and more loudly. Doug actually had to break up an argument between a designer and a salesperson that had become over-heated and was verging on fisticuffs right outside his office.

"I realized that even though we had grown staff and revenue, I was still running the business like it was four people in my live-work loft," he says. That wasn't the case anymore—he had a small downtown office and factory. Yet there was no organization. Doug was making every decision and no one else felt they had ownership over their job or department. "I felt a lack of control, lack of time, lack of money—and I was starting to feel a lack of clients. My business felt like it was diminishing, not growing," says Doug.

Doug met with his five key managers and listened to what they had to say about what was going on in their areas. He looked at the workflow for each project and with his key team focused on how to decentralize and empower managers to coordinate with the needs of other departments. By keeping the agenda tied to client satisfaction there was less griping and sniping and more problem solving. Department heads could make decisions without having to go to Doug with every single problem and question. What could have become an economic nightmare of missed deadlines and lost orders was instead turned around into a more efficient business structure. Now that he was less involved with the mundane tasks of everyday business, Doug was able to stay in touch with existing clients, develop new business, and work on strategy.

Work is more enjoyable for everyone now, and teams act toward a common goal: client happiness. "We now work together with ease because we share one vision and one goal," says Doug. A feeling of abundance and growth abounds in the office and Doug has more clients than ever. The only investment this required was time—Doug had to take a step back and look at what was happening in the business. Today Doug has fifty employees and has branched out beyond T-shirts and tote bags to custom outerwear and home decor. "As long as the structure is in place, we communicate with each other regularly, and people feel they own their jobs, it will work," he says.

With a few simple steps I was able to turn around a chain of restaurants and Doug was able to turn around a business before it started to dramatically deteriorate, without a significant investment of money. Like us, you can turn your flagging business around and make it into a long-term enterprise. It starts with both vision and people. Here are five ways to make it happen on a dime:

1. *Create and communicate a common vision.* The mission of your business has to be specific and accessible to your stakeholders— your employees, customers, vendors, and investors. Everyone needs to be on the same page and working toward the same goals—but they can do that only if they know what those goals are. I described what I wanted to do and my vision of the restaurants' new theme to staff. I did it in such a way that they felt included, which resulted in a high level of buy-in among

workers. I couldn't have done it without their participation, support, and enthusiasm. Doug did it by meeting with his key players and listening to their views on their jobs and the vision of the company. He reached out personally to customers who had been unhappy and pinpointed where the dissatisfaction came from. Key vendors were included in discussions. Only after that was he able to create a structure that addressed workflow issues.

2. *Be upfront and clear.* When making changes to your business, you have to inform those whom it will affect, and you have to be very honest and specific about what you're doing and why. If you don't, you risk losing the trust of those who make your business work. I enlisted the help of the employees at the restaurant. Doug, throughout the process, informed his employees about how he was reorganizing and decentralizing decision making with easy-to-understand graphic flowcharts and other visuals. He held regular meetings in the lunchroom of his offices and made sure to answer all questions about the new structure of the small company. This reduced anxiety among employees and calmed fears that there would be lay-offs. If your plans necessitate layoffs or cost cutting, be honest about it. Don't hide in your office and pretend you're not letting someone go or reducing budgets. That sucks and people hate it—you will lose the trust of everyone around you and they'll leave you high and dry.

3. *Make note of milestones and acknowledge achievement.* Even if you do everything right, change is stressful for everyone. One of the ways you can maintain enthusiasm and momentum among employees, customers, and others is to notice when things go right. Every time you move closer to achieving your

business goals, make note of it and celebrate. When Doug's team made a deadline early, he would send out a congratulatory e-mail blast along with token cash bonuses to the production team handling the project. If the sales team landed a new client, he'd take them out to a casual lunch. Moreover, he made sure to connect each "win" to the overall mission of the company so that the message was clear—the new structure and their shared vision were helping them succeed.

4. *Create an environment.* Creating a good office culture doesn't mean free lattes for everyone every morning, building an employee gym, or having an organic on-site employee dining room. Leave those ridiculous perks to the overblown tech start-ups that implode on a regular basis because of excess spending. A positive office culture is one in which everyone in the company is aligned on values and rowing in the same direction. This is supported by regular check-ins with staff and can be as simple and inexpensive as weekly staff breakfasts, monthly or bimonthly training sessions focused on customer service, an employee-of-the-month program, and simple employee incentive programs. Jody Heymann of McGill University looked at companies with employee-friendly policies, and in a study called "Profit at the Bottom of the Ladder" concluded that "soft" benefits like simple and low-cost employee incentive programs were directly responsible for driving increased efficiencies and productivity among employees. I have long used incentive programs, such as flextime and shout-outs, in the hospitality business and can attest that Heymann's findings are accurate.

5. *Always keep an eye on the future.* As a leader, you have to focus on the future and make sure your team understands this as

well. Obviously, employees need to be attentive to the tasks and deadlines at hand, but they also need to understand that today's successes are part of tomorrow's growth. Company values, regular performance reviews, postmortems after large projects are completed, peer-to-peer reviews, and regular meetings where everyone feels comfortable to contribute all go a long way toward creating a future-oriented team. These all represent no- and low-cost investments with huge payoffs for short- and long-term success.

Bullshit Buster: Sanjay Govil

Sanjay Govil is the founder and chairman of Infinite Computer Solutions, a tech-based business services company. Sanjay worked for IBM and Verizon before establishing Infinite in 1999 with an investment of just one thousand dollars. The company grew with minimal outside funding and had its IPO (initial public offering) on the BSE (Bombay Stock Exchange) and the NSE (National Stock Exchange of India) in February 2010. It was one of the most successful IPOs of that year. Under Sanjay's leadership, Infinite has grown from a single employee, Sanjay in his home office, to a multinational team of more than six thousand employees located in India, the United States, the United Kingdom, Germany, China, and Singapore.

"When I started working in technology it was fairly easy to find a cushy job in a large company and remain comfortable in that environment," says Sanjay. "In 1999 I was working in management for a major telecom company and was doing well in my career. I felt like it was my time to do something else, so I quit my job. I had a family and two children but I had to do it."

Sanjay had an idea for technology-based business solutions in networking, mobility, and other areas, but says he didn't have a business plan. He felt that the idea would be successful because it addressed an issue many businesses could benefit from. "I believe that if you pursue your dreams, good things tend to happen. For me, the plan was to take baby steps." Sanjay had no choice because he had very little money to start—no job and limited savings—not to mention a family to support. His meager one-thousand-dollar initial investment would *have* to be enough. "The one thousand dollars was primarily used to buy a PC and get an Internet connection. I remember getting my first e-mail address but not receiving any e-mails for a long time," he says.

The small steps toward Sanjay's goal of creating an agile tech company helped to ensure that he didn't overspend or overextend himself too soon. "It was important for me to focus on one client, and I made sure I did a very good job there. I wanted to build my references, expertise, and résumé and prove to myself I can grow from one client in a competitive environment."

Once he built up a high standard of results and a range of clients, Sanjay felt it was time to start delegating the day-to-day work. "I did not want to get sucked into the everyday issues of the organization, and I did not want to be the face of the company. If that happened, I would be stuck there forever. One mistake that entrepreneurs make is that they don't delegate to other people. As a result, they get too involved in day-to-day activities and they are not able to use their strengths as the idea person and the visionary. That is the only way the entrepreneur can expand the company."

Sanjay says it is critical as an entrepreneur to realize that you cannot be both the visionary and in charge of strategic planning.

You have to choose, and he believes that being the visionary is more productive for the person who wants to grow and continue to innovate. "Agility is a very critical aspect of a good entrepreneur and a great leader because a lot of time can be spent on mundane matters that are not good for the company. So obviously, process is very important and understanding your environment is equally important," he says. "However, being able to prioritize, reprioritize, and be flexible is the only way to succeed. Having the ability to pivot and adapt to the contemporary environment is paramount."

Sanjay's key advice is that regardless of how much money you make, never lose focus on why you started your business. "Don't forget that you are an entrepreneur first, a person who wants to influence change to better your community," he says. "If you ask Facebook founder Mark Zuckerberg or Amazon chief Jeff Bezos, I would guess they would say that money is not what drives them. I don't think they even check their stock prices. They are focused on making companies better for the good of the people, which is why they are involved in social causes too. Quit mentoring people at your company, quit setting strategic plans; find other people to do those things better than you can do them. These are ways that entrepreneurs limit themselves. In the end, being an entrepreneur is a very simple thing, it is not about money. It is about you exploring the possibilities and finding ways to make a difference and influence change."

Bullshit Buster: Jennifer Myers Ward

Jennifer was twenty-eight years old when she started her online marketing agency in her one-bedroom apartment in Fort Lauderdale, Florida, in 2003. She had to use creative strategies for growing the business and gaining new customers before there was something called social media. "I started the agency, eboveand beyond.com, with only my savings and myself," she says. "Today, there are five of us on staff, and we have worked with dozens of clients in a variety of industries." In 2017, Jennifer's company won the Affiliate Summit Pinnacle Award for Agency of the Year. It's only the fifth time the award has been given, and Jennifer was its first female recipient.

Starting a business wasn't a difficult decision to make for Jennifer, in part because she was young, single, and had no children. "I had a dog, but other than that, I was unencumbered. I also had no idea about the risks involved. I might be more trigger shy today, but then taking a chance on my own business seemed reasonable."

Timing, not resources, was everything for Jennifer. In 1997 she moved to London with no job "just to see what would happen," she says. She had had a job at an ad agency in Charlotte, North Carolina, where she picked up some e-commerce skills, a nascent but growing segment of advertising. However, she hated the ad business, so a change of scenery seemed like a good idea at the time. "Since I had no money, I lived in youth hostels, bought a newspaper, and saw that Amazon was starting to get a foothold in the UK, and it had just acquired Bookpages Ltd., a British online bookseller."

She applied for the job and was hired right away, specifically because she knew a little about the Internet. "I actually had a personal e-mail address. Having an e-mail address, understanding what AOL was about, and knowing what dial-up was got me a long way back then. I educated the higher-ups and talked to the company's clients about the Internet. I had no idea what Amazon or the Internet would become, I was not a prophet, but I was familiar with buying books online. I had enough understanding, more than most people in Europe, of the technology. The online world was the wild, wild West back then. And Europe had to get on board," she says.

After spending three years at Amazon UK, things changed. Jennifer's fourth-year visa was denied because her knowledge was no longer specialized. "I had to either marry a British dude or go home, so I came home," she says. Jennifer was offered a job in the Seattle office, but she didn't want to move to another rainy environment. "I declined the job and moved to Florida where my dad lived. I worked for a brief time at a catalog company in Boca Raton as VP of e-commerce. At Amazon, I had worked with all sorts of products, from tube socks to jewelry, so I knew a bit about a lot of products."

Jennifer stayed with the company for two years, but eventually she realized that even though she loved the work, she wasn't good at sitting in a glass office. "At the same time, friends were asking me, 'Can you look at my e-commerce Web site?' I saw that I was parsing out a lot of valuable information and insight for free. I thought, why can't I do this as a business?"

Jennifer never sat down to write a business plan. "I knew there was a need in the marketplace. I understood what people were not doing right and what they were doing well. I could say don't invest here, invest there. I had the knowledge and no money. But I did have an apartment and a computer on a card table, so I did things that didn't cost any money to get started. I was not in it for the money, but to help people."

Jennifer also overcame a scarcity of financial resources with an abundance of networking skills. The thread that weaves any business is networking, and she attributes a great deal of her success and her ability to start the business with almost no cash investment to a savvy use of the contacts she made and maintained throughout her employment. Jennifer credits the networking aspect of her business for both her client base and her staff—which costs little or no money. "I keep up with people," she says. "I have a drawer full of business cards and I make notes on the backs of them, personal notes about what the person likes, and organize them into different categories. I am also diligent about reaching out to people. When I do reach out I can make it personal because I keep notes. In a week, I talk to at least a couple of people from my card pile."

During her first year in business Jennifer had no idea how long it would last. She noticed there was an eTail conference in Palm Springs, California, across the country from her apartment in Fort Lauderdale. "It cost twelve hundred dollars for the badge, which I didn't have, but I knew I had to be there, because everyone from online retailing would be there—it was like a Grammy list for me." Jennifer didn't buy the expensive badge but she did book a room in the hotel where the conference was being held, booked a cheap flight, and headed to Palm Springs.

Once again, a scarcity of funds did not deter Jennifer. "Everyone socializes at the bar, so I planted myself there. The first day I met people in line at lunch. I made conversation with everybody and met amazing people. One of the guys I met at the bar used to be head of e-commerce at Abercrombie and then The Limited and Things Remembered. I kept in touch with him, and in 2015 I took over his company's e-commerce account from an agency that had had the business for thirteen years! My point is, I met this guy standing at the bar and kept up with him. I followed up on our meeting with a handwritten note. He told me I was the only person who bothered to do that. Personal notes have an impact. They cut through the clutter."

People don't realize they actually have large networks, according to Jennifer, but they should because they are vital to doing business. "You already have credibility with people you know, you don't have to cold-call, and everyone you know knows someone else," she says. "I have never done marketing for myself. My business is all the result of networking, following up, and word of mouth—people saying we do a stellar job. Don't neglect the people you know and meet. It's the most effective and cheapest way to market your business and win customers."

Bullshit Buster: Flora Pringle

When Flora Pringle moved from England to New York City with her husband and baby, she needed to find a way to make money in one of the most expensive cities in the world. She initially hoped to find a teaching job in the city, but quickly realized she wouldn't be able to find a part-time teaching job or cover the insane childcare costs.

Flora wanted to do something worthwhile while working from home so that she could take care of her baby. As a new mother, she became particularly interested in childhood health—especially reading about obesity and the American obsession with sugar. In the course of her research on this topic, she found out about a natural sweetener called xylitol. Xylitol, Flora read, is a sweetener found in fruits and veggies. Our bodies produce it. It's even good for our teeth.

Flora was intrigued by xylitol and thought, what if instead of sugary candies that can cause tooth decay and affect blood sugar and insulin levels, we used this natural sweetener to make a healthy candy that is actually good for people? She decided to experiment with the ingredient herself and bought xylitol inexpensively on the Internet, along with food-grade essential oils, thinking it could possibly be a product with sales potential.

Flora didn't let scarce funds or a lack of experience in candy making stop her. In fact, her naïveté in starting the business actually might have helped her. She used her savings to order ten thousand inexpensive candy tins from China, even as she was still experimenting with her recipe, because she believed so strongly in her idea of healthy candy. "The tins were the only material goods we invested in and we used our savings for that. It was somewhat naïve because when they arrived we were literally living with them under the bed, under the tables, and lining the walls since I didn't have a warehouse," she says.

Once she had the candy—which she called Cracked Candy— figured out, she found a cheap commercial kitchen in which to manufacture it. Having no money for marketing, she went door to door selling her product. "I went to my local stores with my baby in a stroller and said, 'I am a local mom and I have made a healthy candy. Will you try it?' Every store I approached took it on. I got into about fifty stores just by walking into them off the street with my baby and no appointment," she says. "That's how I was able to get Cracked Candy into the Gowanus, Brooklyn, Whole Foods. I walked in and talked to the buyer. Once you are in one store, and have done the necessary paperwork, you can talk to buyers in other stores because they have a lot of autonomy."

The Brooklyn Chamber of Commerce trade show followed, at a cost of just three hundred dollars. "That's where I got my first big client, OTG Management, which runs general stores in airports. They ordered hundreds of tins at a time," says Flora. She hired Brooklyn Community Services, a wonderful organization that provides work for disabled people in local communities, to pack the tins. "That help allowed me to get out of the kitchen, support my community, and sell more and grow the business." When more orders came in than Community Services could handle, she added another packer to her production line.

Flora's success has been led by her ability to see obstacles— her lack of knowledge about the business and her lack of huge funds—as opportunities. And she never lets the bad overwhelm the good. "There were lots of points where I wanted to give up. It's a love-hate relationship. Some weeks you want to walk away, then something exciting happens, like Lena Dunham putting a picture of the candy on her Instagram account," she says. Those things remind me of why I started in the first place, and I'm right back to it."

I hope you now understand that nothing can stop you from going after a goal, starting a business, or making a change in your life. If you get into a business for the right reasons—because you have a passion for it or because you have an idea that will improve people's lives—you can and will succeed. If your motivation is to just make money or hang around with your friends, you're going to fail. If you are not passionate, the only thing you will achieve is mediocrity. There has to be a driving interest and enthusiasm for an idea. Without it, motivation for money or friendship will wane very quickly.

Be willing to take responsibility for failure because that is crucial to your success. Stay on top of the numbers, find the right help, stay agile, don't get bogged down by details that don't matter, and focus on things that create a great quality experience for your clients or customers. That is a formula for success.

You don't need money; you need passion and commitment!

DBY To-Do List

* Just try it.
* If have a great idea for a service or a product, but no funds to create samples or prototypes, do what you can with the resources you have. If you are passionate about a business idea and serious about getting it started, lack of funds is quite likely to be a temporary condition. The adage "Do what you love and the money will follow" has been proven true many times over. It can be true for you too.
* Create a plan.
* Everything I do I start on paper: every promotional idea, every market analysis, and every new creative endeavor. I look at it, digest it overnight, and reread and revise the next day. I see what's missing and what doesn't need to be there. Putting things on paper makes ideas concrete. It is worth the time and effort. I want you to create a plan of action and then systematically implement the plan. Make your idea specific, give it a name, tell people about it, and work on your business every day.
* Get ready to work hard and be creative.
* You have to get in the trenches and make your business happen, especially if you don't have huge funding to hire staff and outsource. The only way to generate revenue is to roll up your sleeves and get to work. Most of the time this means wearing many hats. In the beginning, you have to be willing to knock

on doors, work the booth at trade shows yourself, negotiate your own deals, answer the phones, make your own coffee and lunch, and sweep the floors at night. In short, you might have to be salesperson, lawyer, marketing manager, secretary, cook, and janitor all in the same day. You'll also have to be smart and creative about money and the things that cost money, like inventory and staff.

A FINAL WORD

If you had a dime for every excuse you made, I wouldn't have to be here right now.

Too often I've had to say this exact thing on *Bar Rescue*. I hope you're not going to make me a rich man with your bevy of excuses thanks to our journey together in *Don't Bullsh*t Yourself.*

I do get it, but I don't let excuses get to me. When I don't want to travel another mile for a show, I remind myself of what a lucky guy I am. A middle-aged man with a TV show, a beautiful wife and family, and legions of fans from every age group but especially young people? Come on, Jon, get on the plane! There are not many people who can claim to have all that and more. I earned it, but I'm also an exception to the rule about TV hosts. I always make it to the next gig, and without complaint. Put your life in perspective and you will realize there is no room for excuses.

I believe you can be better today than you were yesterday. Excuses keep us from that because they are the common denominator of every failure. The way to be better every day is to eliminate excuses, and you do that through honesty, professional integrity, and humor. Those three characteristics are evident in every story in this book. I think I've proved that excuses are bullshit, and the truth is, when we own our actions and take responsibility, we have no need for them. I want to leave you with a quick review of the most important and simple tips that can prevent you from falling back on the same old excuses that have been holding you back:

* Communicate with your clients, customers, and staff every day. Reach out, follow up, ask questions, and, most important, *listen.*
* Be present. That means you are working and living in the now. Are you available to talk to people? Are you focused on the tasks at hand, as you should be, or are you distracted by the minor and the unimportant?
* Take time every day, even if it's thirty minutes, to think about your business, come up with or review ideas, and gain personal insight into how your life and business are going. The payoff for this small investment of time is huge.
* Educate yourself—knowledge is power. What can you learn today?

The fact is, when you are working on something important, you try to make it better every moment. That can be frustrating, I get that. So what? Surround yourself with a good team of people who care about you, and do something every day that you can be proud of. Don't let the process, or the ups and downs of trying, frustrate you. Focus on the end result because that's going to be pretty wonderful. Don't be derailed by one more excuse. Just fight it out and you will win.

Good luck! I would like to hear about your experiences. Tell me the excuses you overcame, how you did it, and what happened at jontaffer.com.

Acknowledgments

I did not know it when I started writing, but the stories from the "Bullsh*t Busters" told in this book became my greatest inspiration. In the end, emulating their greatness became critical to me. Thank you all for participating in this book. This book also would not exist if it were not for the amazing owners, managers, and people of the hospitality industry who have taught me my greatest lessons about people, business, success, and failure. To Karen Kelly, who, after hours and hours of listening, always makes me sound smarter than I am. And Mark Itkin, my dear friend who has opened up my professional and personal life so much that this book actually happened. Thank you to my terrific editor at Portfolio, Stephanie Frerich, for her sharp eye and constant support. Larry Ruvo not only contributed to this book, he contributes to "everything." Larry's incredible commitment to community and industry has taught me my most important life lesson, *that my greatest self-fulfillment and purpose come from charity and helping others.* I hope this book helps many. Todd Nelson and his team at

ACKNOWLEDGMENTS

3 Ball Entertainment and Kevin Kay and his team at Spike TV believed in me enough to invest in and launch *Bar Rescue*. Now, six years and numerous episodes later, the quantity and magnitude of my *Bar Rescue* experiences have given me a depth of knowledge that the industry itself could have never provided. You wouldn't be reading these words without my trust and confidence in Leo Squatrito and Team Taffer, who gave me the freedom and time to focus on this book. My daughter Samantha's success in the industry has inspired and taught me so much about the business and about me. I'm so proud of her. My wife, Nicole, spent countless days on the road with me saying "Come to bed" about once an hour as I wrote all night. And last, my most important influence . . . you. Thank you to the millions of viewers and fans who have watched, listened, and read my work. It is all of you who have made me relevant and I am forever grateful. I hope this book delivers for you by causing the actions that move your goals forward.

Notes

CHAPTER 1—EXCUSE #1: FEAR

1. Marcus Luttrell and Patrick Robinson, *Lone Survivor: The Eyewitness Account of Operation Redwing and the Lost Heroes of SEAL Team 10* (New York: Back Bay Books, 2008), 103, 109, 135–37, 276.
2. Ibid.
3. Peter Guber, "Using Stories to Overcome Fear," *Harvard Business Review,* February 15, 2011.
4. Google, "Google Launches Self-Service Advertising Program," Google News from Google, http://googlepress.blogspot.com/2000/10/google-launches-self-service.html.
5. Eric Rosenberg, "The Business of Google (GOOG)," Investopedia, http://www.investopedia.com/articles/investing/020515/business-google.asp (accessed June 4, 2017).
6. Daniel Klaidman, "Navy SEAL Marcus Luttrell Survived the Taliban, but His Struggle Was Just Starting," *Daily Beast,* October 30, 2013.

CHAPTER 2—EXCUSE #2: KNOWLEDGE

1. Calum MacLeod, "Alibaba's Jack Ma: From 'Crazy' to China's Richest Man," *USA Today,* September 17, 2014.

2. Xueming Luo, Vamsi K.Kanuri, and Michael Andrews, "Long CEO Tenure Can Hurt Performance." *Harvard Business Review,* March 2013.

3. Carol S. Dweck, Ph.D., *Mindset: The New Psychology of Success, updated ed.* (New York: Random House, 2006), 3–13.

4. Chris DeRose, "How to Get J. Crew CEO Mickey Drexler on the Phone," *Forbes,* July 24, 2013, https://www.forbes.com/sites/derose tichy/2013/07/24/j-crews-ceo-gets-advice-from-my-wife /#7c3e6e7713a8 (accessed May 31, 2017).

5. Chris Barry, "Putting Social Media to Work," *Bain & Company Insights,* September 12, 2011, http://www.bain.com/publications/articles/put ting-social-media-to-work.aspx (accessed May 31, 2017).

6. American Express, "Good Service Is Good Business: American Consumers Willing to Spend More with Companies That Get Service Right, According to American Express Survey" (press release), May, 3, 2011, http://about.americanexpress.com/news/pr/2011/csbar.aspx (accessed May 31, 2017).

CHAPTER 3—EXCUSE #3: TIME

1. Rebecca Hamilton, "Decisions at a Distance: Effects of Psychological Distance on Consumer Decision Making," *Journal of Consumer Research* 41, no. 2 (August 2014): iii–vi.

2. Frankki Bevins and Aaron DeSmet, "Making Time Management the Organization's Top Priority," McKinsey & Company, http://www.mck insey.com/business-functions/organization/our-insights/making -time-management-the-organizations-priority (accessed May 31, 2017).

3. Fuschia Sirois and Timothy Pychyl, "Procrastination and the Priority of Short-Term Mood Regulation: Consequences for Future Self," *Social and Personality Psychology Compass* 7 (February 2013): 115–27, doi:10.1111/spc3.12011.

4. Brian Wansink, Ph.D., Mindless Eating Web site, Frequently Asked Questions, http://mindlesseating.org/faq.php (accessed May 31, 2017).

5. Wharton School, University of Pennsylvania, "The Importance of Being Richard Branson," *Knowledge@Wharton,* January 12, 2005,

http://knowledge.wharton.upenn.edu/article/the-importance -of-being-richard-branson/ (accessed June 4, 2017).

6. Maxwell Maltz, M.D., F.I.C.S., *The New Psycho-Cybernetics: The Original Science of Self-Improvement and Success That Has Changed the Lives of 30 Million People, updated ed.* (New York: Prentice Hall Press, 2002), 40–42.

CHAPTER 4—EXCUSE #4: CIRCUMSTANCES

1. Christopher G. Myers, Bradley R. Staats, and Francesca Gino, "'My Bad!' How Internal Attribution and Ambiguity of Responsibility Affect Learning from Failure," *Harvard Business Review,* April 18, 2014.

2. Gretchen Gavett, "When We Learn from Failure (and When We Don't)," *Harvard Business Review,* May 28, 2014, https://hbr.org/2014 /05/when-we-learn-from-failure-and-when-we-dont (accessed May 31, 2017).

3. YouTube, Derrick Coleman Commercial Duracell Commercial NFL, https://www.youtube.com/watch?v=buCd72C1oGA (accessed June 4, 2017).

CHAPTER 5—EXCUSE #5: EGO

1. Anjhula Mya Singh Bais, Ph.D., author interview, February 16, 2017.

2. Thelma C. Simpkins, "College at Middle Age," *College Student Journal 14, no. 1 (*Spring 1980), https://eric.ed.gov/?id=EJ217383 (accessed May 31, 2017).

3. Broadway World, "2016 Tony Awards—He/She Said What?! Relive the Acceptance Speeches: Updating LIVE!," June 12, 2016, http:// www.broadwayworld.com/article/2016-Tony-Awards-HeShe-Said -What-Relive-the-Acceptance-Speeches-Updating-LIVE-20160612 (accessed May 31, 2017).

4. Dan Pilkington, "Divided Loyalties," *The Guardian,* February 12, 2007, https://www.theguardian.com/books/2007/feb/12/religion.news.

5. Erzo F. P. Luttmer, "Neighbors as Negatives: Relative Earnings and Well-Being," *Quarterly Journal of Economics* 120, no. 3 (2005): 963–1002.

6. Joshua Correll and Bernadette Park, "A Model of the Ingroup as a Social Resource," *Personality and Social Psychology Review* 9 (2005): 341–59.

CHAPTER 6—EXCUSE #6: SCARCITY

1. Eric Peterson, "Brazilets," ColoradoBiz, July 1, 2008, https://www .highbeam.com/doc/1G1-181733567.html.

Index